"Friend, build your dreams and make them great!
I have every confidence that—with this book—
you are about to turn a corner in your ministry,
a turning with lasting lifetime results.

"It is a turning that will take you from
discouragement and near defeat to optimism and
unexpected victories, from one level of success to another—
to ever higher levels of accomplishment
than you ever dreamed of before you started
real possibility thinking!

"Why am I so sure? Because the principles
of success are all here. Read them. Believe them.
And then apply them!

"They will work, if you work them."

—R.H.S.

Your Church Has Real Possibilities!

by Robert H. Schuller

G/L
REGAL
BOOKS
™

A Division of G/L Publications
Glendale, California, U.S.A.

Any omission of credits is unintentional.
The publisher requests documentation
for future printings.
Photos by Verne Morse

Except where otherwise indicated, Scripture quotations
are from the *Authorized Version (KJV).*
RSV—Revised Standard Version of the Bible, copyrighted
1946 and 1952 by the Division of Christian Education of the
NCCC, U.S.A., and used by permission.
TLB—The Living Bible, Paraphrased. (Taylor) Wheaton: Tyndale
House, Publishers, 1971. Used by permission.
Phillips—The New Testament in Modern English,
copyright J. B. Phillips 1958. Used
by permission of the Macmillan Company.

Second Printing, 1975
Third Printing, 1976

Published by
Regal Books Division, G/L Publications
Glendale, California 91209, U.S.A.

Library of Congress Catalog Card No. 74-84589
ISBN 0-8307-0316-0

Contents

Foreword

Some names come almost as reflex actions. Mention baseball and one of the immediate responses is Hank Aaron. Mention international politics and within seconds Henry Kissinger's name comes up. Mention evangelism and you soon talk about Billy Graham.

By the same token, you don't converse too long about church growth in America these days before you mention Robert Schuller and his Garden Grove Community Church. When the staff of *Decision* magazine, for example, scans the ecclesiastical scene of the U.S. and Canada and compiles a book called *Great Churches of Today,* the Garden Grove Community Church figures prominently.

The field of American church growth is as old as the landing at Plymouth Rock. But the deliberate analysis of the principles underlying church growth in general and the dynamics of specific cases of successful church growth in particular is only recently coming into its own. Probably the publication of *The Bridges of God* by Donald McGavran in 1955 will be recognized as the starting point of the church growth movement. The first phase of what could be called "the McGavran era" took place during the 1960s when research and writing on church growth principles was confined almost entirely to the Third World. However, a second phase is now in full swing, with an unprecedented interest in church growth surfacing in the 1970s in the United States and Canada.

This North American interest in church growth is in no small measure due to the efforts of Dr. Robert Schuller, who through national television, books, lectures and institutes has been calling ministers to "think church growth."

In 1955, the same year Donald McGavran published his book, *The Bridges of God,* 28-year-old Schuller with $500, and his wife as his only member, went to Southern California to test church-growth principles he intuitively felt were valid. He started a church from scratch to test these principles. So, Dr. Schuller has often called his work, "The Garden Grove Experiment." Today, the results of his experiment are known across America as, "The Garden Grove Community Church."

When his concepts and principles for church growth had been proven in the laboratory of personal experiences to be successful, Dr. Schuller chose to share his experience with pastors. In 1969 he organized his Institute for Successful Church Leadership in Garden Grove, California, a truly pacesetting support source to pastors.

One of the distinctive factors of this Institute grows out of Dr. Schuller's conviction of the need for the church to be a *total, balanced* institution. Calling himself a "classical Christian churchman," Dr. Schuller, through his institute equally emphasizes evangelism, education and counseling forms of ministry.

I know of no church leader in America who has kept this all-important balance better than has Robert Schuller in his Institute for Successful Church Leadership.

Perhaps partly because I live close by and have been there myself, I consider the Institute for Successful Church Leadership to be unsurpassed as a church growth training program available today. One of the things that makes it so valuable is that the Institute stresses basic principles of church growth that can be applied anywhere, rather than just saying "this is the method we use to make it happen here." The latter is present, all right, but it is also recognized that some of the methods that are successful in Orange County, California, may not be equally successful in, say, Cold Neck, South Dakota. However, basic church growth principles are effective wherever they are practiced.

Your Church Has Real Possibilities is a book that has emerged from Robert Schuller's institutes. For almost five years these concepts have been pounded into shape on the anvil of dialogue with fellow ministers, tested in the arena of practical experience, and refined in the fires of criticism and response until they have reached the high degree of authenticity and practicality that the reader will discover in these pages. Dr. Schuller's theme, "grow or perish," may be frightening to some churchmen, but it should be a challenge rather than a threat to every one of God's servants dedicated to the fulfillment of Christ's Great Commission (Matt. 28:19,20), and burdened for the 100 million Americans still to trust personally in Jesus as Saviour and Lord.

Robert Schuller's credentials as a successful churchman are impeccable. I have taken the trouble to plot the communicant membership statistics of the Garden Grove Community Church on a logarithmic graph to detect trends not only in absolute growth, but also in *rates* of growth. Widespread studies of many churches have shown that a rate of growth of 25 percent per decade just about keeps up to biological growth, that 50 percent per decade is healthy, that 100 percent per decade is excellent, and that 200 percent per decade is extraordinary. A church growth research team recently studying the San Gabriel Valley (adjacent to Orange County), for example, had a difficult time finding six churches growing at more than 25 percent per decade.

However, the Garden Grove Community Church in the decade 1957-1967 (discounting the first two years which would have made the percentage even higher) grew at the rate of 765 percent, and more recently in the decade 1962-1972, it held at 505 percent. As I write this, I have open before me the beautiful, inspiring artist's painting of the new sanctuary soon to be built to accommodate 4,100 people. The present one, seating only 2,000 will be converted into a dining hall. Why is the church doing this? So Christians will be more comfortable? No. The reason is to make more effective the communication of the living Word of God to 500,000 unchurched people who live within fifteen minutes of Garden Grove. There are no plans for slowing down the growth here.

I admire the vision that sees the task of a local church in those terms. Robert Schuller calls it *possibility thinking*. The author of Hebrews 11:1 calls it *faith*. How this kind of faith, operating through a born-again, Spirit-filled servant of God, has made an indelible impact on the lives of thousands of hurting men and women in Orange County, California; how they have gathered together and formed one of America's great local churches; and how you can apply this dynamic to your own situation comes through in these pages loud and clear.

I highly commend *Your Church Has Real Possibilities* as one of the most stimulating contributions yet to the exciting field of American church growth.

C. Peter Wagner

Fuller Theological Seminary
School of World Mission and Institute of Church Growth
Pasadena, California

July, 1974

Preface

In everything you do, put God first, and he will direct you and crown your efforts with success (Prov. 3:6, *TLB*).

In the strong self-confidence that God has revealed certain techniques for success in our ministry, and in a stewardship of responsibility to share what I have learned with others, I submit my thoughts to you in this book even as I have been offering them in the Institute for Successful Church Leadership.

Hundreds upon hundreds of ministers of all denominations have attended the four-day Institute which we conduct on the campus of our church in Garden Grove, California. As I read the Self-study Guides of these pastors of churches of all sizes and all denominations from all parts of America, I have become acutely aware of enormous misconceptions that are blocking men from succeeding in the work of the pastoral ministry today. At the same time, I feel certain that we have discovered solutions to many of these problems.

There is hardly a church problem that a pastor faces that I have not faced during the years that I have pastored in Garden Grove. I know what it is like to have a dream——only to see it obstructed by negative people. I know what it is like to have a great idea, only to see it crushed by insensitive people around me. I know what it is like to feel an all-consuming ambition to do something great for Jesus Christ, only to find myself hemmed in by small-thinking people; handicapped by no money, no trained lay leaders, no property, no members; and obstructed by an ''impossible'' city planning department and unbelievable building restrictions.

The years have gone so fast that I can still remember the very dark times of my ministry, when I was still in the drive-in theater, and had this magnificent dream of a great glass walk-in, drive-in cathedral. I found myself blocked by obstructions.

For two years I held on through black despair. For almost twenty-four months I went to my office and secretly hoped for a fatal heart attack! My enormous personal pride would never have allowed me to even contemplate suicide. But if God would have removed me with a heart attack, I would have been relieved of command with honor!

I could see no other way out. I held on, clinging to the words of Jesus who said, ''No man, having put his hand to the plow, and looking back, is fit for the kingdom of God'' (Luke 9:62). Then I gave Jesus Christ complete command in the leadership of the church and my life. Obstacles disappeared. The pathway opened brightly. Success was given to me by God. And I know God wants you and your church to enjoy success!

I know that some leaders who read these pages are today in a despairing time of life. I say to you, ''Think with me—from chapter to chapter—and I believe God is going to give you marvelous success, too! I absolutely guarantee that if you will follow the prescriptions laid down in this book, your church will grow. And as your church grows, enthusiasm will mount. Dynamic energy will throb through the congregation. An authentic spirit of renewal will be felt, for such enthusiasm will attract new people.

Try it. And you will soon find that the same dynamic success cycle described herein will be operating for you there in your own home church, just as it does for us here in the Garden Grove Community Church.

Garden Grove, California
November, 1974

Chapter 1

The Institutional Church Has a Fantastic Future

I predict a fantastic future for the institutional church in the United States of America! And in doing so, I realize that my prediction is contrary to much that is being written and offered as opinion by many ecclesiastical theorists.

If I am still alive in the year 2000—and I hope I am—I will be seventy-four years old. At that time, I expect to be addressing a group of young ministers and saying to them:

"It's a thrilling thing to feel the power and the impact of the enormously strong church in America today. Some of you would never believe that in the 1960s and in the early 1970s, leaders of the church were predicting its demise.

"They were gloomily prophesying, 'The church in the future will be away from ground and buildings and into small homes and private cells in communal groups.'

"How wrong they were!"

It will be a thrill to look across America in the year 2000 and see tremendous institutions in every significant city carrying out fantastic programs to heal human hearts, to

1

fill human needs; enormous centers of human inspiration where people rally by the thousands and tens of thousands on Sundays—and gather seven days a week for spiritual and personal growth. These tremendous spiritual-growth centers; these dynamic inspiration-generating centers; these great family-development centers will be proof positive of a renewed, revitalized and resurrected institutional church.

Begin now   Any church that really wants to be a part of this vigorous and vital church of the Twenty-First Century can be. But it won't just happen—that church will have to work at it—and will have to *begin* working at it *now*. How? Through the application of certain universal principles.

Apply anywhere   These principles will work anywhere we work at applying them—they really will. Let us take a case in point of a certain church located on 146th Street in the South Bronx, New York—certainly one of the worst inner-city sections anywhere in this country. If you drew a circle with a half-mile radius around the site of this church, you would enclose eight solid square blocks of deserted buildings, many of them four, six, eight stories high. The windows are knocked out. They are inhabited by gangs concocting Molotov cocktails.

These eight blocks were purchased by the Federal Government some years ago for demolition. The government planned for a brand new model city to rise from the former slum. But what happened? After the government bought the eight square blocks and evicted all the tenants, Congress failed to appropriate the money for the new model city. So the government property simply sits there, eight square blocks of empty buildings that have become a brick-and-concrete jungle.

2

How would you like to have that territory for your parish?

I have been to the South Bronx and to that church. During my visit there, the pastor asked me, "Have you ever seen a 'shooting gallery?' "

"No," I answered.

He took me across the street and to the roof of one of those abandoned buildings. And there I saw cans with blood in the bottoms and perhaps 150 to 200 little white postage-stamp size squares—empty heroin bags—lying around.

"Are there still people here?" I asked.

"Are there people here? This place is full of junkies!" he replied. "They're hurting, and they're scared. They've got problems, but I believe Jesus Christ can save each one of them."

That pastor came to one of our Institutes, and when I saw him, I asked myself, "Why did he come? What we have here won't work for him."

But he got so turned on—so excited—he went out of here believing he had a greater opportunity to serve Christ there in the South Bronx than anywhere else in the United States. He looked at his parish and developed the "inventory" of his community. What kinds of needs did these people have? These needs determined and established the architecture for the building program of his church. He envisaged a building *for people,* not just for an artist. He operated on the principle of biological realism.

Imagine having to seek bank financing in that community! But he did it, and he and his church built a new $700,000 building. No, it isn't the traditional house of worship with stained glass windows. It's a multipurpose facility where basketball backboards hang down during the week. For Sunday worship, the backboards are folded up, and during the services only the reverse sides with the religious symbols on them are seen.

3

That church has been growing ever since its new building went up. But the biggest thing in their entire program is the day-care nursery. The church runs it all week long, because there are mothers there with illegitimate children, and other mothers—if they are lucky—who are working. So somebody else has to take care of the babies, and this is where the church has stepped in. Actually, the day-care nursery helps pay the mortgage, because the city of New York subsidizes much of this sort of activity.

Of course, no two communities are alike, and you have to find out where people are hurting in your community. The theme of this book could be: The secret of a growing church is so simple—find the hurt and heal it!

We have another graduate of our Institute who is the Chinese pastor of a church in the slum section of Calcutta. Now, downtown Calcutta is worse than any city ghetto in America, including the South Bronx! As that pastor sat here in our Institute, I again thought, "Can these principles work for him? He'll go back to Calcutta and then say, 'Yeah, Schuller, it works for you in Garden Grove. But look at all the rich, white, upper-middle class, affluent Americans you've got to get it all together for you.' "

The pastor is neither white nor rich. But he has such a positive attitude. He listened to what we were saying, and then he went back to Calcutta—and went back to work. I visited him there recently and discovered that this pastor now has three churches.

He has one church of about 200 members that worships on Saturday night. I preached there one night, and the place, as usual, was jammed. The next morning we had a second service in a second church. About 300 people attended. Then in the afternoon at his third church, there were about 400 more people in attendance. Three different congregations, three different buildings, three different locations!

Outside one of the churches, I saw pigs roaming the

4

streets, and in those same streets, people slept wherever they could find sufficient place to lie down. There were no sidewalks. Across the street from the church was a large piece of property that had sunk some twenty feet below street level. Its vast crater was filled with foul-smelling water.

The pastor saw me gazing at the eyesore cross the street, and he said, "Dr. Schuller, I use possibility thinking. That's a great big sewage hole now. But one day there'll be a hospital there!"

"But," I pointed out, "you've got a drainage problem there."

"That," he answered, "is an understatement. But what we are going to do is build a moat and then turn that big sewage hole into a little lake with a bridge coming over it—right to the church."

Think positive

Now that's a bright idea. And the pastor is already collecting funds for this project. He'll build it. It *will* be built. It's as good as built now, because he already sees it in his mind.

Many of you have heard the statement, "I've got to see it before I believe it." That's a negative-thinking statement if there ever was one, and it's as wrong as can be!

Believe God

Learn to say it right. Turn it backwards and say, "I've got to believe it before I see it." That's truth! So don't ever say, "I've got to see it before I believe it," because you've got to believe it before you'll see it! You see, it is God at work in us, giving us the will and the power to achieve His purpose. (See Phil. 2:13.)

God doesn't go to work in you to achieve these big, thrilling break-through ideas until you've demonstrated faith. That's how God works, for "without faith it is

5

impossible to please *him:* for he that cometh to God must believe that he is, and that he is a rewarder of them that diligently seek him'' (Heb. 11:6).

"If you have faith as a grain of mustard seed, you will say to this mountain, 'Move...,' and it will move; and nothing will be impossible to you'' (Matt. 17:20, *RSV*). But nothing is more important than faith, and faith is believing it before you see it.

You've got to believe it before you see it! So believe you can build a Twenty-First Century church now! You can be the founder and the leader of such a great new inspirational center. You can make your church a great church for Jesus Christ.

Consider how many years are left between now and the year 2000. Then ask yourself, ''What kind of a job can I do for God between now and the beginning of the next century?''

If you believe it, you'll see it. It will amaze you what dreams He will unfold into your imagination, and it will amaze you even more when He causes those very same dreams to come to pass.

Chapter 2

What Went Wrong in the Church?

How can we have confidence that the future of the institutional church is strong while the institutional church of today is in decline? To understand this, it is important that we consider some of the major reasons for the decline of the institutional church in the mid-Twentieth Century U.S.A.

Until the advent of the Second World War, the United States of America was a small-town and city-oriented country. The institutional church was represented largely by the "First Church Downtown on Main Street." The unfortunate thing was that you would find a First Presbyterian Church on one corner, a First Methodist Church on another corner and a First Baptist Church kitty-corner to the other two!

After the Second World War, America moved into the age of suburbia. With the new rise of suburbs around the major cities of our country, Protestant leaders of all denominations formulated some basic policies for church planning which were to determine the destiny of the institutional church for several decades.

The key church planners from various denominations realized that we were now facing a new opportunity in the history of the church in America to develop a church in the rising suburbs in such a way as to avoid the mistakes of the past. But at this point there were certain assumptions unchallenged and unanimously accepted by church planners; assumptions which formed the basis of a catastrophic policy for church extension and development.

Let us look at some of these assumptions:

1

The "large" church is bad news.

Witty, brilliant, but cynical comments made the rounds such as, "The large church isn't a church — it's a ranch!"

The church planners assumed that the ideal size for a church was approximately 500 to 800 members. Putting it another way, "The ideal church is about 150 to 250 families. This is just the right size for one pastor to handle effectively."

Why? Why did the church planners assume that the large church — with several thousands of members — was ineffective? To understand that question, we must remember that mid-Twentieth Century America had been living in the tycoon age. All large institutions and establishments, with rare exceptions, were tycoon-generated, tycoon-motivated, tycoon-managed, tycoon-administered and tycoon-promoted. You could tell the name of the company by the tycoon's name: Ford, Chrysler, McCormick, Goldwyn.

The same form of administration and management was obviously at work in the huge churches that existed in our nation until this time. The problems of the tycoon-centered church were conspicuous. When the tycoon died, the churches for the most part turned out to be huge, empty auditoriums. So church leaders formulated a hasty assumption that "large churches are bad."

Oddly enough, the mid-Twentieth Century saw a change of emphasis, as well, in the industrial and business world. Stockholders could see the terrible shortcomings of tycoon management. But, unlike the church, they never considered breaking up the large industrial enterprises. They saw the positive values of hugeness. And they simply used their creative imagination to dream up solutions eliminating the negative aspects of "bigness." And thus was born "team management," replacing "tycoon management." Today the masses of large companies of America are headed by teams of competent senior executives whose names are not household words.

The business world during this period was saying: "Let's look at the values of bigness and devise ways and means to eliminate the basic negative aspects of great size." As a result, the industrial empires of America have merged together, creating larger markets, pooling resources and achieving greater success.

But the church has reacted negatively to "tycoon management" by saying: "All big churches are really bad news. We will control planning for the future in such a way that we will have no large churches."

It was during this time that I graduated from seminary, accepted an assignment with a small church in Chicago —and began ringing doorbells. I soon found that as the pastor of a little church I did not have the program to appeal to the masses. All we could offer was a big Sunday School with one "adult" class. We had scarcely enough young people to make the group large enough to be exciting. We didn't have enough good musicians to have a good choir, so we urged people to sing in the choir who were really not at all talented.

I also found in my small Chicago church that I had nothing for the single adult or the young college kids or the divorcees. If only we had several thousand members, I thought, we could have large and effective groups for every type of human being. Unquestionably, I saw the large church as the most effective church in the mission of evangelizing the non-churched people. So, when I was given the opportunity to come to California in 1955 to begin a church on my own, I leaped at the opportunity!

I am totally convinced of the advantage of the large church today and feel that it is the church for the Twenty-First Century. So what is the result of the false, unchallenged assumption that big churches are to be avoided?

The result is that the denominational leaders in church planning formulated a variety of goals based on this premise. For instance: If the ideal church is 500 members, then you would need only about an acre of ground. The sanctuary could be planned to seat 300 or 400 people. A few classrooms and one office would suffice. And so across the country in all the new suburbs, property was secured—in the early developmental stages—of one acre on an average, occasionally two or three acres, and rarely, perhaps five acres! As a result, new Protestant churches sprang up across the country designed to be small. And, for the most part, they struggle and limp along today!

One pastor is an ideal arrangement.

Obviously this is a most unintelligent assumption. Even a cursory observation would indicate that the average ordained pastor is not a ten-talented man. He may be a good preacher—or a good pastor—but he is generally not strong in both areas. He may be a good pastor but not skilled in organizational work. His appeal to the youth or to the educational department of the church might be strong or weak. Perhaps he is a good pastor and even a good preacher, but very ineffective as a promoter and as a finance planner. Or perhaps his strength is in counseling and in no other area.

10

It remains incomprehensible that intelligent church planners could assume that ''a single pastor arrangement is the ideal arrangement.'' Yet this is precisely what must have been assumed. For a 300-seat sanctuary, on one or two acres of ground, with 500 to 700 members could expect to generate only enough income to support one full-time minister, perhaps a full-time secretary, some part-time help, with a little money left over for missionary activities.

3

The church should be "in community."

This meant that, ideally, the church should be located in the center of a square section of developed land. Perhaps across the street from a junior high school! The tragedy is that this is precisely where the newly developed churches of the mid-Twentieth Century sought and secured their ground. Untold thousands of churches are located today off the beaten path, with masses of persons living in surrounding communities unaware of their existence, that is unless, they happen to have a child in the neighboring junior high school! This assumption that the church must be ''in community'' was related to another unchallenged assumption of the church planners: that a square mile of newly developed suburban homes would adequately support a church.

Church planners, immediately after the Second World War, would drive through bean fields, corn fields and wheat fields, watching the new houses spring up by the hundreds. Overwhelmed by the mass housing developments that surpassed anything they had seen before, they assumed that 1000 new homes would be enough for one large church! Certainly, then, one square mile of ground which would be turned into approximately 2000 to 3000 homes would be more than enough to support a single church!

After only a year in the pastorate, I had done enough

doorbell ringing to find out that this assumption was totally erroneous. Half of the people in any community were already loyally committed to a faith.

The church planners failed to realize that if even 50 percent of the people were committed to a faith elsewhere, that left only about 1,000 uncommitted families. And these, for the most part, were the disenchanted or disinterested who couldn't care less about the church. The half that remained would be tough to win! The odds were stacked against success.

The church planners also assumed—and wrongly so—that if there was one Protestant church in a square mile, it followed that every Protestant residing in this square mile would attend that one church! They forgot that some loyal denominational followers would go outside of that geographical area to a church of their own denomination—and that they would drive three, four, five, six or more miles to get there!

4

Parking is not really very important.

Pastors of new churches complained about the fact they had to spend money to buy another acre of ground to meet the city planning commission's requirement of one off-street parking space for every five seats—or something of the sort.

Now, the parking requirements varied from city to city and community to community. But what did not vary was the negative attitude of church planners and the local pastors toward the off-street parking regulations. I know. I was unanimously in accord with all of those who complained about the fact that we had to spend so much money to park cars off the street.

Elaborate cases were prepared by pastors for planning commissions, arguing that "one parking space for every five persons was unnecessary. Did not the great churches

12

through the years succeed without parking, other than along the curb?"

And so it was not uncommon to see many new churches develop in the mid-Twentieth Century without any parking provisions whatsoever! We were yet to discover that if a church were to grow, it must have surplus parking.

Churchmen can communicate effectively through preachments, commands, orders and pronouncements.

On this assumption, prominent church leaders in their national and international assemblies preached their sermons in the form of pronouncements. They sent them down to all the people on the grass-roots level expecting them to accept, perhaps debate and then improve situations because of these divine declarations!

This method may have worked in the Roman Catholic church twenty years ago. And it may have been effective in many Protestant churches a generation ago. But today we no longer assume that we can communicate with people effectively through the preachments-pronouncements approach. Why? Because we now recognize that this form of communication is essentially insulting. It assumes that the party making the pronouncement or the person giving the sermon is the more enlightened, intelligent, informed, brilliant or sensitive party.

Such a form of communication is hardly a compliment to the man on the receiving end of the pronouncement or sermon. Consequently the pronouncement form of communication establishes polarizations, creates chasms and establishes a mental climate where effective, warm, meaningful dialogue becomes a virtual impossibility. So whether they are in a pulpit, in an international ecclesiastical assembly or in a religious convocation, people who want to succeed in communication will avoid the pronouncement approach.

Rather, instead of issuing pronouncements, we should

be communicating through the witnessing approach. An enthusiastic sharing of what God is doing is the way to communicate with people and change their lives. We may witness, or we may ask questions. The "question-approach" form of communication builds bridges where dialogue becomes a genuinely constructive reality. What a contrast to the pronouncement approach!

The successful communicator today attempts to put every communication objective in positive terms that are designed to stimulate the positive emotions in the hearer. Then he knows if he "sells his idea" by stimulating the positive emotions, he will not only have a solid convert, but a happy and enthusiastic Christian as well. The result is a Christian who has investigated, questioned and come up with satisfying answers which he is thrilled to pass on to others. So you see, successful selling is nothing more than communicating to people a truth that they weren't aware of before!

Big-time denominational labels impress people.

For myself, I was and still am affiliated with the little denomination called the Reformed Church of America. And it was widely felt by many of our new church pastors that if we had a name like "First Presbyterian" we would really be able to impress the non-church people!

What we *did not* realize was the obvious: that *unchurched people are not impressed by denominational names*. If the non-church people were impressed by the name Presbyterian, Methodist, Baptist, Episcopalian, Lutheran or whatever, they would at this point be members of such a denominational church!

Great churches give 50 percent of their income to "missions!"

So almost all new churches started in suburban America were made to feel that they were "selfish" if they didn't quickly strive to give more and more to "Na-

14

tional Headquarters.'' In church after church I discovered pastors without secretaries, mimeographing their own bulletins—in order to ''save money for missions.'' Yet I could not find one denominational executive that did not have secretarial services!

So the home offices tried to skim off the first meager profits from their new branch offices instead of urging them to concentrate for the first ten years on ''reaching every unchurched person in the community—your *first* mission!'' It's no wonder that today national headquarters are lacking in income. They stunted the growth of their young by demanding too much too soon! Better to have 10 percent of the mission dollar income of a large church than 50 percent of the $50,000 income of a small, stunted church.

The real result of these assumptions was the loss of regional power bases. During the mid-Twentieth Century, the large ''Old First Church,'' long the sturdy, solid, power base of the region, declined along with the decline of the old downtown where Old First Church has been for years. *So the large old churches declined downtown while no master plan was prepared to replace these strong centers of power with new, equally large —or larger —power centers in the newer suburbs!* By default, as we have seen, suburban churches were designed against largeness!

Result of assumptions

Too few master church consultants, if any, really understood the enormous value of the large old churches on Main Street or the three vital functions they had served:

Three vital functions

They formed a strong financial base.

15

They were the largest churches and, in most instances, the wealthiest. Thus they generated a mood of financial strength, security and confidence to the regional group of denominational churches: "Old First will back us up!"

They were sources of enormous psychological power to the smaller churches and to struggling pastors in the region.

In a sense they served as "psychological cathedrals," as strong father-figures providing a sense of security to all small churches in the area. To the smaller congregation which could denominationally identify with the large Old First, there was a "sense of belonging to something bigger and stronger than myself!" This kept the little churches and struggling pastors from despair, even as a weak left hand does not contemplate severing itself in suicide from the body, but rather draws security knowing that it belongs to a larger, healthier organism that can support and sustain it!

These Old First churches were centers that became reservoirs of human resources for great lay leadership.

Here lay leaders were found who could spearhead the great lay movements: the building of a youth camp, the underwriting of a religious radio program, the launching of an evangelistic crusade and many other major projects.

So, throughout the history of Protestantism in the United States, we have always had large churches that were the financial, psychological and human-resource power centers of the region. They were the sturdy base-blocks in the regional denominational foundation. But they were undervalued, apparently. Negative thinkers only saw "what-is-wrong-with-the-big-churches."

Thus it was, that with the dying-out of Main Street with

its large churches, together with the development of suburban churches *designed against largeness,* a weakness penetrated the institution. For the new churches managed to grow only strong enough to pay for their own pastor's salary, make a token contribution to benevolences, and maintain a mediocre Sunday School and inadequate Youth Program.

By the beginning of the 1970s, up and down America, Protestantism began to discover that they were without power centers in many regions! In this state of affairs, young and struggling pastors and churches had no strong Father Church figure in their area to look up to for emotional strength! So younger churches and pastors became discouraged even as the pastors of Old First Church downtown became discouraged.

It is no wonder that in this state of affairs, the established institutional church slid into an era of inferiority complex. It declined and tended to be judged—falsely, I must add—as a dying and ineffective institution. This paved the way for other new and irresponsible concepts based, once again, on untested, equally false assumptions like "the institutional church is dead"—or the prediction that the church of the future will be the underground church or the church in the home!

Again, such irresponsible predictions neglect the obvious: *only an established church with buildings, people, staff and program can form a base of operations for generations to come.* Eliminate the church, the established power base with its buildings, its ground, its parking, its staff, its program—and you eliminate the base of operations for the future! This would be comparable, in the Second World War, to an attempt by the Allies to invade Europe without having England as a power base from which to launch the attack!

The tragedy is that the unchallenged assumptions which shaped church extension in the mid-Twentieth Century, U.S.A., were and are assumptions that violate the fundamental principles of successful retailing.

Much as it may offend many leaders in the Christian church, the truth remains that the parish church is in the business of ''retailing religion.'' We define retailing as ''bringing the goods and services to the consumer,'' in contrast to wholesaling which packages products or ideas but doesn't deal directly with the customer. In that sense the national church headquarters and theological seminaries might be called wholesalers, while the local church is the retailer. So we had better discover the secrets of successful religious retailing!

Chapter 3

Seven Principles of Successful Retailing

In the mid-Twentieth Century, the era of church extension, the Protestant churches moved into the suburbs to build their new pretty little places on too-small pieces of ground—snugly hidden from the masses of people on the move in their swift cars. In this same period, the business retailers moved from the downtown main street, now dead and defunct, into the suburbs to lease space in exciting new retailing developments called "shopping centers."

The birth and rise of the shopping center retailing development is one of the phenomenal successes of American business in the Twentieth Century. All successful shopping centers meet the basic principles for successful retailing, which are as follows:

1

Accessibility

Shopping centers are located at major highway interchanges or at the junctions of major streets or highways. Logically, the first thing a businessman needs is a good road to his place of business. It is obvious that the best product cannot be sold and will not be bought if people

19

can't get their hands on it! So, in putting the church within the heart of the community, the church was violating a fundamental principle of retailing—accessibility.

A second principle for success in retailing is surplus parking. Forward thinking planners talked about "ample" parking. And it is obvious from my review of hundreds of Self-Study Guides from hundreds of churches across America that very, very few churches have *ample* parking. By ample parking, we mean off-street parking spaces for the faithful members of the church who could be expected to attend on an average Sunday.

Successful retailing, however, demands far more than *ample* parking. Successful retailing demands SURPLUS parking! With the development of the shopping centers with their acres of *surplus* parking, modern Americans became used to this convenience. And as they have become spoiled by easy parking afforded by the shopping centers, they have become more and more disenchanted, impatient and irritated by the parking congestion they find elsewhere, including that in their own church settings.

Now, the *faithful* had, and still have, a high tolerance level. But if a non-churched person decides to visit a church on a particular Sunday and drives up to the church only to see the entire parking lot filled, with cars parked along the curbs in every direction, the odds are that this person will simply drive on. His body and mind are conditioned by his life-style throughout the week.

In the middle of the week, if he decides to go out to a restaurant for lunch and heads for the Red Lion, only to find the parking lot filled with cars and all the curb spaces taken, he will anticipate that the restaurant is "jammed and service will not be too hot." So he simply moves on to the Black Bull and pulls into the parking lot where there is an empty space.

20

Now his behavior pattern, shaped by parking as he knows it in the business world, is not going to radically change on Sunday when he comes shopping for a church—unless he is deeply committed. And the non-church person whom we ought to reach is not deeply committed at this stage! Surplus parking is an absolute requirement for successful retailing.

To any pastor, I make this firm declaration: if your church does not have surplus parking, you are hurting. You are paying a high price for this lack of parking! It would be much cheaper for you to buy additional property, to build a high-rise structure, or to sell out and relocate on larger property. It would be less expensive for you to do this, with a 20- or 30-year loan, than it would be to struggle along in a dying way as you are today!

We faced this problem in our church when our ten acres became too crowded for two services. Our parking lot was entirely filled with 700 cars, and cars were parked along the curbs. We believed that we had to have surplus parking. As a result, we were determined, if need be, to build a high-rise parking garage. We discovered this would cost five dollars a square foot. At that rate, we concluded it would be cheaper to buy an adjoining ten acres of ground zoned for costly commercial purposes. We did secure ten additional acres at a cost of a million dollars, or only $2.50 a square foot! And we have all the frontage rights, street rights and air rights as well.

As soon as we purchased the additional acreage, we increased our parking to 1400 cars, and the growth of the church with this additional *surplus parking* was phenomenal. Attendance rose astronomically! We discovered that many older people had stopped attending church *regularly* when they felt they might not be able to find parking space. Many of the faithful began to become less *faithful* when they began to worry about finding a place to park. Surplus parking, I repeat, is an absolute requirement

21

for successful retailing in America today.

I feel so strongly about surplus parking, I would say it is the number one criterion that must be met in order to grow. The truth is, you need surplus parking before you need pews! You may have a beautiful sanctuary, with marvelous pews and a gorgeous organ and a fantastic choir and an exciting preacher, but if people can't park their cars, they will never stop and come in.

The opposite is also true. If there is surplus parking, they will stop their cars, they will attend services, and a certain percentage will remain if the program is effective. The first thing you need, before anything else, is surplus parking! Get them to park their cars, put their keys in their pockets, and you have them for a Sunday morning!

The third principle for successful retailing is inventory. If I am out shopping for a shirt, I inevitably head for a particular department store. It is located in a shopping center right off the freeway, which means it's easy to get to. I know I can always find a parking space without driving around and around and around. And I know they will have the shirt that I want: the neck size, the sleeve length and the color. Time is too valuable to waste making a trip—only to find they don't have the goods. Customers will go where the business has a reputation for having a wide inventory range.

This is precisely the problem of the small church. Too many persons find that the church, small and beautiful, "just doesn't have what they are looking for." Perhaps they are single adults in their twenties and there is no program for them! Perhaps the church expects them to join the *one single adult* group which includes people in their forties and fifties! Or the unchurched family is suddenly beginning to get interested in finding a church that has an exciting youth program. The church that is large enough to have the inventory to meet almost every conceivable human need is a church with a fantastic future!

The next principle for successful retailing is service. Accessibility, getting to the place; surplus parking, providing a modern convenience; and a good inventory—all of these are principles for successful retailing. But ultimately the service department is what will make the retailers succeed year after year after year. If you purchase an item and find out that the business will let you down when you need it serviced, the odds are that you'll be slow to go back there. They may lose you as a customer.

Does your church give good service? Remember, you

have to have the service. And, in the churches, that means a trained laity. You can't have a successful church without trained lay people.

The job description of our key staff men is *to recruit, train and motivate the lay people* to call on the unchurched, to keep calling on people after they've joined the church, to telephone and counsel the people who have problems, to do the work of education. That's what is often called the "enabling ministration." And it's also called service!

5

Visibility   Your church needs visibility. You have all these things: accessibility, parking, inventory and trained service people. But you have to have visibility, too. People who need what you have also need to know that you're in business and that you've got the product.

If they don't know you're in business and don't know that you have what they need and want, obviously you can't help them and you're not going to grow. This means, among other things, that you have to advertise. It's amazing how the Holy Spirit can use advertising power!

How much of your budget is spent on advertising? Please notice that we are discussing principle 5. After all, you can't advertise unless you've got the product and the inventory first. And you can't over-advertise.

I don't think there's a church in America that spends more on advertising than we do—or have. Personally, I've had a lot of exposure, press coverage, television interviews, radio time—all of these. No church has been more photographed than our Tower of Hope in Southern California. But we know we are not over-advertised.

A couple of years ago I took an airplane from New York to Los Angeles and then took a limousine from the International Airport to the Disneyland Hotel in Anaheim. From the hotel, I took a cab to my home in northwest

Santa Ana. I didn't know the cab driver, and as we were driving along the Santa Ana Freeway, I thought, "I'll have a game with him."

So I asked, "What's that big building over there with the cross on top?"—pointing to our church tower!

Do you know what he replied?

"That's a Catholic hospital," he said.

"How long have you been driving a cab?" I asked further.

"Seventeen years."

"Where?"

"Right around here in Anaheim and Garden Grove."

Imagine that! A cab driver in our immediate area for seventeen years, and all along he thought our church was a Catholic hospital!

I tell that story often, and at one of our Institutes a young minister taking a cab back to catch his plane home decided to play the same game with his cab driver.

"What's that big building with the cross on top?"

The driver told him, "A mortuary!"

Unbelievable!

Visibility—they've got to know you're there, know what you are and know that you have what they need and want.

Possibility thinking

Even if you already have the other five principles operating for you, you still need possibility thinking in your church leadership.

What is possibility thinking? It's having the right value system, asking the right questions and making the right decisions. You see, once your value system is straight and clear, you simply reduce it to the right questions. Then decision making is easy.

In our case, our value system is service to Christ and our fellow men. And we've reduced our value system to three questions. Let's say somebody in our church gets a great idea. On our church board it is heretical for anyone's first question to be, "What will it cost?" Why? Because we're not in a profit-making business. That's not our value system.

But we do ask three other questions:

Would it be a great thing for God? If we get an answer "Yes," we move to the second question:

Would it help people who are hurting? We ask this because if we think it will only be a great thing for God and will not really help people who are hurting, then it is probably a pie-in-the-sky, pietistic, heavenly-minded, but-no-earthly-good idea. Besides, if it doesn't really meet a practical human need in the here-and-now, you probably won't be able to sell it anyway. You will not be able to make it go.

If we get a "Yes" answer to those first two questions, we ask the third question:

Is anybody else doing the job? If they are—forget it! Help them, cooperate with them, but don't compete with them. That is, unless they are doing the job in such a clumsy, ineffective way, or they don't want to cooperate with you. Then, if you know you could come in and do the job right, okay, do so.

Those three are the only questions we ask. That's possibility thinking leadership.

After we get the right answers to these three questions, what do we do? We make the necessary decisions and go on to find solutions to the problems involved. That's possibility thinking leadership.

Remember, indecision can fatigue you to the point where you will not be able to think or dream up solutions to problems. I believe it is better to make a wrong decision than to make no decision at all. Why? Because if you make a wrong decision and learn from it, you will make another decision—a better one.

26

You dream, you make a commitment. You dream, you make a decision. That's possibility thinking leadership. Believe it is possible. Inch by inch, anything's a cinch. And all you need to get started are ideas, good ideas.

Although money is never the first problem to be faced, it is obvious that to succeed in retailing you need good cash flow. I want to say something at this point about financing: *don't be afraid of debt, but understand what debt is!*

Let me illustrate this point from my own experience. When I left Western Seminary and went to my first pastorate in Chicago, Illinois, I lived in the church parsonage. It was heated with coal, and when October came, I needed coal for the furnace. One of the men in the church said, "Well, it'll take about five tons of coal to get you through the winter. At fifteen dollars a ton, that's seventy-five dollars."

I didn't have seventy-five dollars so I called up the coal yard and asked, "Will you deliver five tons of coal?"

"Yes."

"Will you charge it, please?"

"Oh, we don't charge coal."

"You're kidding!"

"Oh, no, not at all. Guess you'll have to borrow it from the bank."

I hung up.

At the bank, I asked, "Would you loan me money for coal?"

"Oh, no," the banker replied, "we don't loan money for coal." What he didn't say, and what he meant was, "You're only twenty-two years old and you're new at all this, so you don't know any better." Then the banker said, "I tell you what, Rev. Schuller. I'll loan you money for coal this time, but never again."

27

"Why not?" I asked.

"Well," he explained. "You will burn up that coal. If you don't pay us back our seventy-five dollars, what do we get in return? Nothing—it's all gone up in smoke."

That banker then gave me some of the soundest advice I've ever received: "Never borrow money for coal. You want to borrow money for a car—for a house—come to us. And all we will say is, 'Can you make the monthly payments?' If you've got the cash, or the salary coming in to make the monthly payments, we'll loan you money on that house or car.

"Then if you can't pay the mortgage back, we take the house or the car and sell it. If there's any money left over after we get paid, you get it. We call that equity.

"But," he went on, "never borrow money for the gasoline you put in the car. Never borrow money for the tires you put on the car. Never borrow money for the spark plugs. *Never borrow money for coal.*"

Now that's a fundamental principle. We borrow money for this church, but we don't borrow money for coal! We borrow money for everything that has collateral, non-depreciable value. But we don't borrow money for our television ministry, for interest on the capital debt, for salaries or for utilities. That's coal money. That's gasoline. That's tires.

Before you borrow money to expand, build up your income to the point where you can afford to borrow the funds. This means that you must build up your cash flow base so that you can at least be sure you can pay the interest and the utilities of the expansion. If your cash flow is built so you can handle these items, then you can expect the added crowds that come—because of the expanded service—to take care of the capital depreciation of the principal.

Follow these procedures, and your net worth will go up! And then you will not really have any debts. You will have liabilities, but you'll also have a positive net worth. Our church has about 2.9 million dollars in liability. But we also have a net worth that is over a million dollars!

Raise men and you'll raise money!

Waldo Werning, perhaps the foremost authority on church funding said it: "Raise men — lift them up! Inspire their spirits! And they'll support your ever-increasing cash needs!"

What I have told you here is, in essence, the financing cash flow of the program we use in this church, and it's been successful. But to achieve the same success, you must also maintain these same disciplines. Do so, and you'll find the solution to your church money problem and cash flow problem.

It is true, by the grace of God, that some churches are enormously successful without meeting these basic retailing principles. It is also true that no church can be permanently successful by ignoring these fundamental principles of successful retailing.

I have sometimes described the Garden Grove Community Church as "a 20-acre shopping center for Jesus Christ." We are located right near a freeway interchange, with acres of surplus parking, with the buildings and the inventory in the form of a program and service designed to meet almost every conceivable need that an unchurched person might seek and expect from a church.

We have not been without our critics. But the truth is, our church program has continued to grow by leaps and bounds while those who have criticized have declined astonishingly.

We are not trying to prove to anyone that we are right. We are only trying to help every other minister in the Church enjoy the same success for Christ's glory that has been ours in His happy work!

Chapter 4

Grow or Perish

It is a law of life that "where there is no growing, there is dying." Where there is growing, there is dynamic living. The church must either grow or perish.

But are you sure you want to grow? The tragedy is that too many churches really do not want to grow any larger than they already are. Let's look at the kinds of churches that do not want to grow:

1

The small church with entrenched lay leaders who fear they will lose their positions of power if they win the dynamic leaders in their community.

The old guard that forms the power structure of the church may lose their power position if new blood comes into the membership of the church. It is a tragic truth that many little churches in the country will not grow because their leadership, in the hands of entrenched power groups, would consider their own positions threatened.

Here is a story that has unfolded too often. Some young pastor comes to begin a new church in a new community. Beginning with no members, he is eager to receive whatever support he can secure at the outset. No wonder that he enthusiastically reaches out and grasps in gratitude the first men and women who move forward to offer their help. And, again in most such cases, the first people to move forward and offer help are men and women who have never before held positions of influence or leadership in a church.

I think of one particular congregation that is represented in our files of hundreds of churches that have come through our Institute for Successful Church Leadership. Let us call this the Case of Church 127 in a midwestern suburb of a great city. The church organized with forty-three charter members. A church board was formed with twelve officers—elders and deacons and trustees. Not a single one of these twelve men had ever been a member of a decision-making, policy-setting board of directors before. Not a single one among this group demonstrated anything other than a notch over failure in private life.

Now, suddenly, the power of the church was in the hands of twelve men who felt strangely and terribly important. But they lacked the vision, imagination, courage and the determination that makes for qualified and dynamic leadership. Because they were both inexperienced and insecure, they were natural obstructionists to their young pastor. With enthusiasm, he would call from door to door, from house to house, winning the interest of non-churched people who then attended his services of worship, only to receive a cold shoulder from the newly entrenched "Charter Church Board Members."

The chairman of this church board was employed as an attendant in a gasoline station. He looked upon the school superintendent who visited in church one Sunday as someone who would certainly be elected to the chairmanship of the church board if he should ever become a member of the congregation. It is not surprising that the

31

school superintendent never joined the church—nor did the village doctor, nor a successful salesman, nor a dynamic insurance executive. All were made to feel unwelcome by the entrenched leaders for fear of the loss of their power positions. The truth is—they didn't want their church to grow!

If this were an isolated incident, it would not be so upsetting, but unfortunately this is all too common. I recall one young minister who attended our Institute for Successful Church Leadership and who wrote me shortly after returning home. He was quite unhappy. He complained that he was "more depressed than ever." He pointed out that he "failed to really find the help to make his church succeed."

I called for and studied again this man's Self-Study Guide. He was, I noticed, pastor of one of nearly forty churches in a town of slightly more than 7000 population. The location of his property was certainly not desirable. The church lacked parking. And worst of all, simple market research would indicate that there simply was not room for another church in this community.

The Self-Study Guide revealed no potentiality here for growth. The town had no prospect of increasing population in the next ten or twenty years. I wrote him a letter and asked him one blunt question: "Why was your church ever organized in the first place?"

His letter came back reeking with regrets. "Dear Dr. Schuller," he wrote, "when you asked why we got started in the first place, you touched a very tender nerve. Several families who were active members of a local labor union were accused of violent militancy in a strike. As a result, the church where they held membership threatened to discipline these parishioners who were jailed for a weekend because of their union activities. The offended militant union members promptly removed themselves from the congregation, went to this neighboring town, arranged to make a small down payment on a little church building and proceeded to organize their own church."

Naturally, this congregation was hesitant to welcome any strangers into its fellowship. But knowing that they would have to grow in order to survive economically, they looked for a dynamic young minister and persuaded him to come. Yet they refused to open their hearts genuinely and sincerely. No wonder the church does not grow. Lay members of this church do not want it to grow!

Are you sure you want to grow? If you do, and if such a condition hindering growth exists, strong leadership must be forthcoming. The congregation must face up to its insecurity; and must, through a renewed discovery in Christ, be willing to open itself to new members.

2

The church infected with negative piety.

Afraid that they might lose their purity, fearful that somebody might come into their ranks who is not truly "born again," this church—made up of super-pious, holier-than-thou, narrow-minded persons—does not dare to grow.

Shockingly and surprisingly, I can report that there are hundreds and hundreds of such congregations in our country. Somehow, the church must discover the power of the Holy Spirit to do His converting work in human life. It is amazing how successful the church has been in creating obstacles, building boundaries and carving chasms between the community of Christians and the non-churched people.

By contrast, it is so refreshing to live and work with Christians, in a church relationship, who look only for sincere love for Christ and a warm commitment and devotion to Jesus Christ as a criterion for membership. Beyond a doubt, extreme narrow-minded piety, with man-made regulations and restrictions, has been an ace card used by the devil himself to keep potential converts out of the Christian church.

The church that labors under the "we're big enough already" theory.

There are still untold tens of thousands of pastors and lay leaders who believe the unchallenged assumption of mid-Twentieth Century church planners who propagated the notion that 150 families is "just the right size." Suddenly, an arbitrary numerical figure establishes and controls the program and policy and future of an institution! The idea surely must have been dreamed up in the mind of the devil himself.

It is contrary to all the natural and spiritual law to form an arbitrary figure as the ideal size for a church. To do so is as unnatural as to take an *ideal* size shoe and tie it on a young child's foot so that the foot will never become larger than the "ideal" size. We have all read what happened to the feet of Chinese women generations ago who were deformed by this crude and dehumanizing growth-restricting concept. Likewise, the church that is forced to remain small by a preconceived notion of what makes a nice-sized church—such a congregation is doomed to become disfigured and dead.

One thing is certain: *a church must never stop growing*. When it ceases to grow, it will start to die. And when it stops growing, it will cease to hold its dynamic leadership. Its staff members, if it is a multi-staffed church, will look for other positions which offer a challenge, adventure and excitement. Dynamic, effective, energetic and successful laymen, as well as professional churchmen, gradually drop away from a non-growing situation. And finally, the church realizes that in losing its dynamic leadership, it has allowed the seeds of death and decay to be planted.

**The church that
literally has a
fear of growth.**

Of course, growth will mean problems. Growth will mean more buildings have to be built. Perhaps the adorable sanctuary with the stained-glass windows will become too small. "We certainly wouldn't want to sell it, would we?" Or, "We certainly wouldn't want to get involved in having to build a larger sanctuary which would mean *raising money!*"

Growth does produce problems! But these problems are the very challenges that generate energy and vitality that mark an institution as being *alive*. Where growth problems do not exist, death lingers near!

Fear of growth rises also in the minds of some pastors. There are not a few churches that are led by insecure ministers who really do not want the church to grow for fear they might have to add additional staff ministers to the organization. And, indeed, there are not enough ministers who have learned the skill of working in a multi-staffed situation. But certainly any minister who honestly searches his heart and concludes that he does not really want his church to grow for fear he will have to add additional staff ministers and perhaps share his glory, his weddings, his funerals and his baptisms—such an insecure pastor must come to stand afresh before Jesus Christ and surrender himself once more to Christ as his Master, his Lord and the Leader of his church.

Now, are you sure you want your church to grow? Believe me, it can—unless you are in Newkirk, Iowa, or some other such place with a declining population. There are very few churches that we see in our Institute for Successful Church Leadership that do not have growth potential! Consider the pastor of a beautiful New England church who attended our Institute. The old colonial chapel was a community landmark in the old downtown square. It was and is a historical landmark. It was and is a magnificent example of pure colonial architecture.

Unfortunately, the growing population in the city offers fantastic opportunity for this church to grow—except for one thing: the existing edifice is a growth-restricting problem. The church conducts two services of worship and already is filled. They obviously cannot grow as long as they continue to use this beautiful structure. As a result, the church board has virtually adopted a no-growth policy. The question was addressed to me in a counseling session: "Dr. Schuller, what should we do?"

Our suggestion was to retain this magnificent facility as an inspirational place of worship in the city center. Retain it as a chapel for weddings, small funerals, special baptismal services with recorded devotional programs to be played in the sanctuary throughout the week—with the doors open to tourists and residents to enter for inspiration.

Meanwhile, the congregation was encouraged to move its major church operational and functioning plant to a new piece of property approximately one and one-half miles away. Here, on a new 10-acre parcel of land, a large sanctuary can be built—with a large educational and recreational plant, a dynamic youth center, with generous off-street parking and the physical capabilities of a sanctuary—a plant designed to accommodate a maximum membership of 4,000 people in the next twenty years. This plan is currently under consideration and, when adopted, will produce fantastic excitement, energy and an enormous future for this church.

This much is certain. Where there is no potential for growth, there is great potential for death. *Grow or perish!*

Chapter 5

Eleven Growth-Restricting Obstacles

Let's take a look now at eleven growth-restricting obstacles that are holding back Protestant churches in America today. Based on our Institute's research into static and declining churches, we find ten attitudes that are preventing many churches from moving ahead. Check these obstacles to church growth and see if any of them exist in *your* church:

1

Most churches that fail do so simply because they never really planned to succeed! The spirit of comity, or cooperation, began in the cooperative Protestant ecumenical movement with the best of intentions. As new suburbs were developed across America, Protestant churches of the main denominations agreed that, at all cost, we should avoid mistakes of the other generations—such as having four different denominational churches on four corners of a downtown interchange.

The idea that "it just happens" without cause or effort by the church and its leadership.

37

Now, with new cities being developed across the country, we had a great and grand opportunity to start new churches, placing them a mile apart. This sounded wonderful. The only problem was it then assumed that each church had one square mile of free territory. It assumed that competition is always sinful and destructive. It overlooked the fact that competition is frequently a creative and fruitful goal and causes pastors and lay people to really get out and work!

One minister in our community said to me when I came to start our church, "Schuller, starting a church here is like shaking ripe fruit off a tree. I'm the only church in one whole square mile." When he opened his first unit, it was quickly filled with people. He was overwhelmed by 200 people crowded into an auditorium which seated 150! Immediately he was struck with the false illusion that this was easy and virtually effortless. Unfortunately, that church—quite predictably—failed because of his attitude at the outset.

There should, indeed, be no hostility, proselytizing or undermining of another church. But the cooperative spirit that causes any church to relax becomes failure-prone. I frequently tell people that "I work as if our church were the only church of Jesus Christ in all of Orange County and the salvation of all the souls depended upon us alone."

Now I know full well that there are hundreds of beautiful and wonderful churches in the county that are proclaiming the gospel as effectively, and many more effectively, than we are. But if all churches took the attitude that they, and they alone, were responsible for the whole county, the entire non-churched populace would be so overwhelmed by the dynamism, the energy, the vitality of the body of Christ in its witnessing movement that conversions would take place by the thousands!

It is still true that too many pastors in too many churches talk a different language from the men in the street. The pastor's vocabulary is theological, academic and overly orthodox.

One need only look at the average hymn language and understand how meaningless much of the theological language is. "Seraphim and Teraphim" are familiar words from an old, old hymn. But what in the name of seraphim do these words mean to non-churched people?

Assuming that we successfully bring unchurched people into our Sunday morning services, will they understand what we are talking about? If they are biblically illiterate, will they understand the biblical terminology? And if they fail to understand, will they not turn off?

2

The church's detachment from the world.

Many churches are so dignified they're dull! The music is dull, the messages are dull, the architecture is dull; there is no excitement in the air! The worship service might be described as sleepy, quietly meditative and a perfectly tranquilizing arrangement—guaranteed to produce yawning and boredom.

There is absolutely no excuse for the bearers of the good news of the gospel of Jesus Christ to be anything but enthusiastic, exciting and dynamic! If the gospel is truly preached, it will be preached as *exciting* good news! Good news is never dull. If a service is dull, there must be no good news. If there is no good news, there must not be any gospel!

3

Boredom

The pastor who emphasizes fear, hate and anger instead of faith, hope, love and joy has an emotional problem!

4

Emotional ailments

in the lives of
pastors and lay
leaders.

The congregation that needs to hear sermons that stimulate the negative emotions of fear, hate and anger, instead of responding enthusiastically to rejoicing sermons that stimulate the positive emotions, such a congregation is neurotic! The parishioner who does not leave church complimenting the pastor, unless the sermon has been delivered with a red face and glaring eye, must be a sick person! We cannot expect people to rush in to overflow the churches that generate fear and anger.

5

Success

I know a minister, pastor of a Methodist church, who started his young congregation in a growing suburb and organized with a membership of 157 persons after five months. It was so exciting that he said to me, "It's a thrilling work!"

I asked him, "How many of the 157 members transferred from other Methodist churches?"

He answered: "One hundred fifty of them."

I shuddered. I felt that this pastor was depending upon his denominational strength to produce members in the years to come. He knew too well that he belonged to a denomination that numbered its national membership in the millions. The possibility of hundreds of Methodists moving into the growing community in the next ten years was great.

Today that "successful" church has nearly 1000 members. The tragedy is that it should have 3000 members! It was an instant "success" because of its denominational pull.

But if you depend on transfers for the growth of your church membership, you are doomed to die! No church deserves to grow or to live unless its purpose is to win non-churched people to Jesus Christ.

When I arrived in Garden Grove in 1955 with my wife as the only other member I remembered that I belonged to a small denomination of only 200,000 in America. I calculated that in ten years I could expect no more than seventy people from my denomination to move into this territory. Therefore, we would never grow unless we could successfully impress and win 50 percent of the people living in the community who were totally unchurched. This lack of strong denominational backing proved to be the first and greatest blessing our church ever received!

Yes, success can be your obstacle.

Debt consciousness

A fear of increasing indebtedness has kept one church from deciding to borrow the added money to enlarge its sanctuary and improve its parking problem. As a result, the church has not increased but has declined in growth and consequently declined in income. If an institution faces a strong growth potential, it almost always pays to borrow the money to expand immediately! Unfortunately, the mortgage burning ceremony becomes in churches what the gold watch and retirement papers become to the retired person—a symbol marking the end of productivity.

Our policy has been to borrow as much as we could, as fast as we could, to meet needs as quickly as we could. But be careful now and understand what I am saying.

There are some guidelines which are most important as you borrow money:

First, never borrow to the extent that it will whittle away your net worth. Your net worth must always be growing, so as to provide a sound financial base on which to operate.

Second, never borrow money to pay for interest on debt. Before you increase your corporate debt, broaden your financial base to demonstrate a regular cash flow that can at least pay for the added interest cost of the proposed increased debt.

In other words, if you needed another $200,000 to build classrooms or offices and the interest on that new debt would be 10 percent then you would have a campaign to increase your weekly income at least $400 to pay the added annual interest. The cash to reduce the principal could—in most instances—be expected to come from the increased growth resulting from the increased service offered by the expanded facilities built with the increased debt.

To borrow dollars to pay for interest is a proven path to bankruptcy.

Third, never borrow more than you can amortize over a 20-year-period. In our budget we have a figure we call debt service. That figure extended over twenty years would totally pay off all our indebtedness.

The truth is, financial debt frequently is a spur to church growth. Members of the church know that their support is needed there—and people need to be needed. As a result, they do not resist maximum contributions. And where their treasure is, there will their hearts be also.

The files of another church reveal a 22-year-old institution that, for all practical purposes, is a dead church. It had good growth at the outset, continued to increase steadily until it was ten years old, then leveled off. Growth came to a standstill at that time because the two church services were virtually filled and this meant that there was no longer surplus parking.

About this time, I was called in by the pastor to offer my advice on their developmental planning. I recommended that they contemplate borrowing $200,000 which, at that time, could have been secured at 6 percent interest over a 20-year period. The $200,000 was to be used to build a sanctuary to seat 700 people and to increase their parking by 250 cars.

The response of the church board was, "But we have a $50,000 debt now. We have to wait until we get that paid off, then we will think about borrowing more money." The result was that the church failed to keep up its dynamism. The community got the impression that the church was no longer growing—as, in fact, it was not. The church got the reputation of being static—not moving, not going anywhere, not doing anything—and consequently growth tapered off.

Now, many years later, the debt is paid off, but the attendance has also declined. The dynamic personalities within the church that made it grow in the beginning moved away in discouragement and attached themselves to institutions that were more alive and aggressive.

Debt consciousness and the fear of debt can kill a church. In the case at hand, the borrowing of another $200,000 would have increased the budget by only $16,000 the first year, enough to cover the first year's interest payment. This would have amounted to a little more than $300 a week. There is no doubt that the enlarged sanctuary, with the additional parking, could easily have brought in $16,000 in the first year!

7

Doubt and confusion in the 50s and 60s

Not a few pastors and lay people began to question the reality of God and the authority of the holy Scriptures. The only institution that can grow is the institution that is totally convinced of its ministry and its message. No salesman can sell a product unless he is thoroughly sold on it himself first! No church will grow if it is not uncontrollably enthused about its faith!

8

Distractions which have diverted energy and

There is no doubt that the pastor of the church must be responsible in offering community leadership. He should be the conscience of the community. The church that exercises its evangelism without seeking to relieve social problems is a lopsided institution.

But church historians may well record that the church in the late 1950s and especially in the 1960s was overly involved in social and political activities to the utter neglect of its mission of seeking to bring the good news of Jesus Christ to non-churched people in the community. In every age and every historical phase, there have been fashions and fads that could easily distract a pastor or his people from their primary mission, which is to preach the good news to hungry hearts.

Arthur F. Burns, chairman of the Federal Reserve Board, said at Los Angeles on December 7, 1970, while explaining the near disastrous inflation of the 1960s: "Many businessmen became so preoccupied . . . that they lost sight of the primary business objective of seeking larger profits through improved technology, marketing and management. *When talented corporate executives* devote their finest hours to arranging speculative maneuvers, the productivity of their businesses inevitably suffers—and so does the nation's productivity."

Wise words! During this same period, our finest churchmen were preoccupied with "glamorous," "fashionable" and "speculative mergers and maneuvers"— distracted from their primary objective of winning the 100 million Americans who are not Christians!

"To merge two old, declining, denominations is NOT growth!" I declared when in the 1960s the Reformed Church in America was considering merger with the Southern Presbyterian Church. "Take two old, insecure people and let them marry. It may be a beautiful idea but don't expect the union to be fruitful with new children!"

The
controversial
pulpit

Controversy has been a major cause of membership

44

decline in Protestanism. There is a proper time and place for the church to deal with controversial theological, political, social, biblical issues. But the pulpit is seldom the right time or the right place for the following reasons:

First, the fact that an issue is controversial means that sincere people disagree. Every person deserves to be treated respectfully even if you disagree with him. And you insult his dignity if, behind the shielded protection of a pulpit, you authoritatively challenge his position without—in fairness—giving him a chance to ask questions or share his viewpoint.

And if you ever insult the dignity of a person, that person will not be converted, he'll only be inflamed. At best he'll walk out and never return. At worst he'll become a bitter enemy.

Controversy should only be handled in a setting (like a classroom) where no person feels he's being indoctrinated without a chance to ask honest questions. In the disastrous sixties two words were "in words" by many churchmen. They were "confrontation" and "dialogue." Crazy! For confrontation always results in polarization and a mental climate where dialogue becomes impossible! Little wonder church membership plummeted!

10

Short-sighted leadership

Probably the foremost obstacle to church growth that comes to light as we study the hundreds of Self-Study Guides in our Institute for Successful Church Leadership is what might best be termed "short-sighted leadership."

Three-year and five-year pastorates are common, if not average. As a result, the average church has no 10-year plan, no 15-year plan, no 20-year plan. Personally, I shall be forever indebted to Dr. Raymond Lindquist, a former pastor of the First Presbyterian Church in Hollywood, who lectured at the seminary when I was a theological student. "Boys," he said, "never take a call to a church unless you can envision spending your life there.''

When I came to Garden Grove, it was with the belief that this field would hold enough opportunity for my energies to be released fruitfully for years to come. As a result, I laid out a 40-year plan.

I was twenty-eight when I began the church. My denominational constitution suggested sixty-eight as a retirement age, leaving me forty years to work in this field. What could I possibly do if I gave forty years of my energies to one church?

When you have that amount of time, you can start to dream big. In the same manner, an artist who is told to imagine a painting that may fill a canvas 100 feet long by 20 feet high is going to envision a far bigger picture than an artist who is given a canvas only 8 inches by 12 inches in size!

11

Impossibility thinking

Undoubtedly the most widespread obstacle to success, both inside and outside the church, is what I choose to call ''impossibility thinking.'' Jesus Christ said, ''If you have faith as a grain of mustard seed, you will say to this mountain, 'MOVE hence to yonder place,' and it will move; and nothing will be impossible to you'' (Matt. 17:20, *RSV*). You would suppose then that the Church Christ founded would be packed with possibility thinkers! While men of the business world and in the scientific community have been shooting for the moon, the Protestant church has been inflicted with impossibility thinking.

In an earlier book, I define impossibility thinkers as ''people who make swift, sweeping passes over a proposed idea, scanning it with a sharp, negative eye, looking only for the distasteful aspect. They look for reasons why something won't work instead of visualizing ways in which it could work. So they are inclined to say 'No' to a proposal, never giving the idea a fair hearing.

46

"Impossibility thinkers are people who immediately and instinctively react to any positive suggestion with a sweeping assortment of reasons why it can't be done, or why it is a bad idea, or how someone else tried it and failed or (and this is usually their clinching argument) how much it will cost! They are people who suffer from a perilous mental malignancy I call the impossibility complex. They are problem imaginators, failure predicters, trouble visualizers, obstacle envisioners and exaggerated-cost estimators!

"Their attitude produces doubt, stimulates fear and generates a mental climate of pessimism and fatigue. They are worry creators, optimism deflators, confidence squelchers. The end result? Positive ideas buried, dreams smashed and projects torpedoed."[1]

The solution? Somehow, Protestantism must experience a revival of possibility thinking! The belief that we are co-workers with an Almighty God who can accomplish anything that would be a great thing for His cause in this world!

Footnotes

1. Robert H. Schuller, *Move Ahead with Possibility Thinking* (New York: Doubleday & Company, 1967), pp. 14–15.

Chapter 6

Leadership: The Crisis and the Crying Need

There is no substitute for dynamic, aggressive, positive, inspiring leadership! Almost without exception, the lack of success means the lack of effective leadership. And the reverse is true. Great success is the result of great leadership.

Recently I returned from a visit to the Taegu Presbyterian Hospital in Taegu, Korea. I have never in my life seen a more successful Christian mission in operation than this work that is going on under the dynamic leadership of Dr. and Mrs. Howard Moffett. More than 150 churches in the area of Taegu have been started and nourished by the ministry of this hospital. And all of Korea is aware of this exciting ministry.

The hospital itself stands as one of the great medical centers of the world. Multi-storied and fully equipped with the latest modern medical devices, the hospital stands as an inspiring example of doing something in a big way, with a spirit of excellence. Many millions of dollars have been invested in this ultramodern missionary venture.

I also think often of the Christian Medical Center in Vellore, India, a fantastic success story which gives great honor and glory to the enterprise of Jesus Christ on earth. At Vellore, just as at Taegu, the secret of success is dynamic leadership. One person, Dr. Ida Scudder, inflamed the minds of people and got them behind her amazing project.

It is thrilling to see something done *right!* Too often, Christian enterprises have been guilty of doing too little, too modestly and too late. We are not always like the old army general who explained his successful mission in this classic sentence: "We always were the firstest with the mostest!"

Leadership is the key to church growth. If the church is to really succeed in its mission of witnessing effectively to the non-churched world in the Twenty-First Century, we must develop dynamic, aggressive and inspiring leaders. *Leadership is the key*

And what is leadership? Leadership is thinking ahead, planning for the future, exhausting all possibilities, envisioning problems and dreaming up solutions to them, and then communicating the possibilities and the problem-solving ideas to the decision makers. *This* is leadership.

In any institution, the leader is the man who is thinking ahead of everyone else. He is not living in the past but in the future, for leadership draws its inspiration from future projections and not from past accomplishments. The leader is alert to movements, trends and evolving developments. He is literally thinking longer thoughts than anyone else is—and expressing them effectively!

49

Who is the leader in the modern American church? As we look for the answer to this question, we shall uncover some pretty unhappy situations. And we shall offer some suggestions on who *should be* the leader in the local congregation.

In our consultation with many ministers from different denominations through our Institute for Successful Church Leadership, we have discovered a real leadership crisis in the modern Protestant church. There is confusion as to who really is supposed to be in the leadership role.

Some ministers assume that the leadership of the local church must come in the form of ideas, theories and practical suggestions from their denominational executive officers. In such instances, the pastor is often not the dynamic and creative leader that a local situation demands for a successful mission. The local pastor who looks to a national executive officer for leadership is seldom the dynamo that a local church needs for exciting forward movement.

It is obvious that national directors of denominational bodies cannot be in touch and in tune with every local situation. How can they possibly be expected to be effective leaders for each local church? The social, spiritual and community needs vary drastically from one community to the next. Consequently, the leadership role must not be detached from the local setting. Those who head the administrative work of major denominations may be the official or unofficial "bishops" of the local pastor, but except in rare instances they should not attempt to be the proxy leaders of the local congregation.

We find other ministers who expect that leadership is vested in the heads of the theological seminaries. Somehow, a local pastor expects that ideas for effective churchmanship should be forthcoming from the theological schools. It is our contention that the role of the theological school does not afford a sensible setting for inspiring local church leadership.

The theological seminary must necessarily deal with such weighty matters as theology, church history and other top level projects. Again, the theological professor is prone to be lost in his own mental world of academics and tends to be detached from the heartbeat and the soul throb of the people who live within the radius of the local church. Generally speaking, a local pastor who goes to a theological seminary and expects to receive inspiring leadership for his church program is looking in the wrong direction.

Leadership is full time

Perhaps the bishop—or whatever your church calls him—of the diocese or the district or the synod should be the inspirational leader. Is this where the root of leadership is to be found? The bishop, like a national executive director or a professor of a theological seminary, can doubtless provide much needed wisdom and valuable direction. But the local bishop cannot be the leader of the local church.

Leadership is a full-time business. A local institution needs a full-time leader who can be thinking, planning and selling his ideas; a man who can be solving the problems that stand in the way of the successful achievement of local goals.

Is leadership then to rest in the local church board or in the local congregation? We find several churches that are struggling alone and labor under the illusion that the congregation is to be the "corporate leader." These churches with a strong congregationalism allow no major thinking, planning or promoting to be done without congregational approval. If the pastor and the church board feel they need to buy new hymn books, they would expect to call a "congregational" meeting for the approval of such a decision.

I have yet to see a church with such a system of government that is really roaring ahead with fantastic success! In this type of system there is no room and no authority for strong, inspiring, centralized leadership. And whether we like it or not, this kind of leadership is the key to successful church development. Any dynamic, progressive and enthusiastic pastor will find his style being cramped, his energies draining away and his dreams turning into despair if he thinks he has to "sell" his plans and his dreams to a negative-thinking congregation.

Is the church board then the corporate leader of the church? Perhaps the board is the "corporate" head and the pastor is the "errand boy" to carry out the church board-prescribed duties? To answer this question, let's look at how effective modern business operates while, at the same time, remembering the words of our Lord who said, "The children of this world are...wiser than the children of light" (Luke 16:8).

In a growing, modern American industry you will find a board of directors. This board, for the most part, consists of wise advisors who are part-time thinkers. They meet occasionally to approve major propositions of their leader. They are a consulting group that the leader uses to test out his ideas before they are publicly launched. When they approve the ideas of the leader they hired to dream dreams and then to plan and execute them, they look upon their role as supporters—to sell the decision to the community that needs to get behind the program.

In such a case, who is the leader? Leadership does not rest with the board of directors. Leadership rests in the hands of full-time executives who are hired by the board to think ahead, plan ahead and envision great possibilities, as well as ways in which these possibilities can be profitably exploited and ways in which potential problems can be solved. Leadership then rests in the hands of full-time, salaried people.

If I were a capitalist financing an enterprise, I would insist that the unchallenged leadership be placed in the hands of full-time thinkers and planners. As a pastor heading up a church, I insist on the same.

There will be no great forward renewal in the Protestant church until we recognize that dynamic and aggressive leadership is the key. Leadership definitely does not belong in the hands of part-time thinkers. So the place of leadership logically and naturally rests in the lap of the minister and the salaried staff leaders in the church!

Leadership is responsibility

Leadership is an enormous responsibility that cannot be irresponsibly placed in the hands of people who do not put the church first in their lives. And no matter how dedicated the members of a local congregation are, the church does not take first place in their lives. The same can be said for members of the church board.

The most dedicated elder, deacon or trustee—with rare exception—considers the church to be the third priority in his life. His business, career or profession is generally first interest, with the welfare of his family second. The church comes third—and perhaps not that high. In many instances, his hobby takes third place and the church has to settle for fourth in his order of priorities. But the local pastor places the church foremost in his life!

Let there be no dodging of this issue. Pastor? Do you hear me? You should be the spark plug. You should be the inspiring commander leading the troops up the hill!

I recall that when I was a seminary student, working part-time in a local church, the pastor told me: "Never forget, Schuller, that you are a servant of the church and not its master. The consistory (the church board) is the leadership group. They do the planning and the deciding.

You do the work. They will tell you what to do. Carry out their orders faithfully and you will be a successful pastor.''

I was enormously impressed by this misguided advice. As I look back on it, I remember attending board meetings in that church where the board was the leadership group and the pastor their "faithful servant.'' I recall sitting in a board meeting where two hours were spent discussing whether or not they should buy a new sump pump for the basement of the church. It is incomprehensible that twenty-five minds could spend two hours wrestling over such a petty decision!

Leadership is thinking big

Big things happen to big-thinking people. Nothing big ever happens to little-thinking people. Important movements are started and carried out by big people who are able to make vital decisions swiftly and move forward with confidence and assurance. This can only happen with positive leadership in control.

Leadership is organization

In the Garden Grove Community Church, the leadership rests in the hands of the pastor and his professional staff. The church board approves the basic policy and then expects the ministerial and professional staff to take over the job and move it ahead with maximum effectiveness.

Let me illustrate how this works.

In the early days of the church, I presented the budget to the entire congregation for its approval. It was a terrible mistake! There was always *some* member who could find *some* fault with *some* item in the budget. There is always going to be someone in the church who doesn't appreciate the music and doesn't want the money spent to buy a good organ or to build up a topnotch choir.

What we were doing was simply creating a public

platform for negative thinkers. We quickly abandoned the program.

Our budget is now prepared by committees. In a large, multi-established church such as ours, a full-time salaried person is usually the liaison person on each committee. I am the minister who virtually controls the publicity committee. It has always been so, except for a two-year period when, we lacked the bylaws to give me leadership power. Then a negative-thinking minority in the church succeeded in manipulating appointments to the publicity committee so that one of their friends who opposed advertising was made chairman. As a result, for that period of time I couldn't get a dime to advertise.

Since then a new set of bylaws gives me, as Chairman of the Board, power to appoint committee chairmen. I insist upon this. So I have since had control of publicity. It is an area where I am capable, so my leadership is not challenged.

The minister of education is the staff man on the Christian education committee. The minister of youth is the staff man on the youth committee. The business administrator is the staff representative, along with me, on the finance committee. So it goes. A professional salaried member of this staff is in close contact with each committee.

Meanwhile, as the president of the corporation and chairman of the board, I, as senior minister, am an ex-officio member of all committees and appoint the chairmen of all these committees to the church board for their approval. By appointing the committee chairmen, by being an ex-officio member of each committee, by being the chief of the staff presiding over regular staff meetings, I am able to maintain leadership control over the entire operation of the church, working through the church board, committees and staff.

It is our sincere belief that this is the only way to organize a church for successful leadership. In a church with a smaller staff, it simply means that the senior pastor would attend more of the committee meetings himself instead of entrusting the flow of leadership into committees through one of his staff members.

Does this mean that the senior minister is a dictator? And that he and the staff, who are hired to run the church, are the big bosses? Not at all! The senior minister is not a dictator for the following reasons:

1. He is hired by the church board or the congregation.

2. He reports to the church board and the board reserves the right to overrule his recommendations.

3. He appoints the chairmen of the committees, but the board must approve these chairmen. And, in our church at least the chairmen of the committees are always selected from the board itself.

4. The minister can only *recommend* and *launch* the project. Obviously, the success of any program can be effected only by loyal, hardworking and generous-giving laymen and laywomen who pick up the ideas of their leader and make them work!

I have often said, with utmost sincerity, "I have never done anything in Garden Grove Community Church. The people have done everything!" And they have! I have done a lot of possibility thinking, a lot of possibility planning, a lot of mental problem-solving—and a lot of talking. But it's the board that makes the decisions. And it's the board that disseminates possibility thinking throughout the congregation to infect the entire membership with the inspiring conviction that the ideas that have been adopted are tremendous.

Great things will happen in a church where big-thinking lay people will say to their pastor, "Pastor, we want you to spend all of your time dreaming great dreams on how our church can become the greatest mission for Jesus Christ in this whole territory! And, pastor, show us how we can get behind your big dreams and make them succeed. We will

(1) be praying for you through the week while we are earning the money to pay the bills to make this dream come true; (2) we will also welcome training to equip us to do the actual work of the church as lay evangelists, teachers and counselors!''

Pastor, be an analyzer; be an organizer; be a climatizer—and you will be an inspiring leader. *Analyze* the needs and potentialities of your church and your community. *Organize* the program, the staff and the plans for making the church move ahead. *Climatize* the people through your positive and inspiring sermons so that they will want to get behind your dreams and make them come true.

Leadership is leading

You, pastor, must be the leader, under God, reporting to the board! That's God's call and command to you!

Where does leadership rest in your church? The tragic fact is that in a majority of churches we've seen in our Institutes, leadership has been surrendered to property. The size of the structure and the location of church property sets the pattern for everything they do. Leadership—that is, the thinking, programming, planning, goal setting—is not in the hands of the church board nor the congregation, nor is it in the hands of a bishop or a denominational leader, nor is it in the pastor's hands. All are prisoners of the property that they own—or rather, that owns and controls them! The shoe must never tell the foot how large to grow!

This means God Himself has lost control. For God can think through a brain but God cannot think through a brick! So great dreams are never born here—''We wouldn't have room to park the cars,'' ''We couldn't seat the people,'' etc., etc.

Ninety percent of all American churches should relocate! That's the impression I have after examining the

57

Self-Study Guides of thousands of protestant churches!

"It's time that the leadership be changed!" I must often advise pastors. "You take command. You have the freedom to sell that property! Release yourselves from bondage! Break loose from the chains that bind you. Break forth into the freedom of dynamic leadership! God cannot be the leader of a church if the creative imagination of human beings is blinded and bound by glass, stone, plaster and dirt."

Many pastors have followed our advice. Church properties have been put up for sale. Extensive acres of land in prime locations are being purchased. And the pastor, the board and the congregation are now being inspired by God to do something great! God is in command again!

Leadership of the church is not to be placed in the hands of part-time administrators or people removed from the scene of action. Nor is leadership to be controlled by a piece of real estate, a bank account, a treasurer's report or a denominational manual.

Leadership is to be in the hands of a living human being who is constantly thinking, constantly praying, constantly reaching out and constantly surrendering himself to the Holy Spirit of Christ. That, my big-thinking, possibility-thinking pastor, is YOU! Now make up your mind to be the leader. Assume your responsibility and build a great church for Jesus Christ!

Chapter 7

What Makes a Truly Great Church?

Years ago a fellow clergyman asked me: "How many members do you have in your church, Dr. Schuller?"

I answered, "You just made three mistakes in that one question. First this isn't a church—it's a mission. Second, it's not *mine*—it belongs to Christ. Third, we don't have members—they're all ministers and only a few get paid."

Read through this chapter and you'll understand why I answered as I did. For a truly great church is first of all a mission!

I was trained in Reformed theology. For my B.D. thesis in Western Theological Seminary in Holland, Michigan, the faculty approved my project to prepare "a scriptural and *exhaustive, theological, topical* index to the four-volume *Institutes of the Christian Religion* by John Calvin. I had no idea how big a job it was going to be! Nearly 300 pages long, it at least made me an authority on John Calvin's theology.

I discovered then that the theology of the Protestant reformers was, to some degree, reactionary. Calvin's definition of the church was "a place where the word is proclaimed, sacraments administered, and discipline maintained." The definition ignores emphasizing the most important aspect of the church—which is "a group of joyful Christians happily sharing their glorious faith with the despairing souls of their fellowmen who have never known the joy of Christ!"

The church   Now let's see what constitutes a great church and then lay down the pattern for organizing a great church!

The church is a corporate group of happy Holy Spirit-inspired Christians who allow themselves to be minds through which Christ can think, hearts through which Christ can love, hands through which Christ can help. In that sense, the church is the living body of Christ, *helping* hurting people in a local community. And nothing is more exciting than to be a part of the body of Christ in its caring, sharing love.

If you were to come to Garden Grove Community Church on an average Sunday, you would see magnificent buildings, remarkable crowds—and you would witness inspiring services of worship. You would probably leave the church enormously impressed, commenting, as many visitors have: "What a great church this is!"

The truth is, of course, that beautiful buildings with spacious grounds do not necessarily mean that the happening is a great church. My particular job as senior pastor is, hopefully, to deliver messages that will bring great crowds to church on Sunday morning. And as the leader, it is my job to organize the institution in such a way that this enormous crowd of worshipers becomes a true and vital church.

By all means do not allow yourself to be confused by

the anti-organization people. They love to say, "The church is an organism not an organization." The truth is: *every organism God creates is always organized!* The nose always is on the head! or else the creation is a chaotic mess.

I am the first to declare that a great crowd of happy Christians gathered in a place for public worship does not make it a church! It might be a "Preaching Center." In another case it might be an "Evangelism Center." In still another case it might be a "Camp meeting," a "Bible Conference," a "Missionary Rally" or a "Charismatic Conference Center."

There are in America today not a few dynamic organizations where large crowds of Christians gather in one place once a week—or more—to sing or pray or study the Bible. Often these large assemblies of people are loosely referred to as "churches." Part of this confusion is the result of the different schools of thought that train the Protestant pastors.

There are in America educational institutions called "Bible Institutes." Historically they have been efforts to extend beyond his lifetime the work of an evangelist, i.e., a person whose really only single concern was to "save souls." He had little interest in the nurture of these souls other than to "put a Bible in their hands."

Hence Bible institutes emphasized evangelism—how to get people saved, which usually meant getting them to come forward and kneel at the altar in a public service. Further courses taught there would be on song leading, prayer life, personal witnessing and Bible study. From the perspective of the typical Nineteenth and Twentieth Century traveling evangelist this was all the education a person needed to go out and "preach the gospel."

Then there are the training centers called theological seminaries, most of whom belong to the American Association of Theological Schools. Every "main-line"

American Protestant denomination has these training centers for ministers. The thinking behind the theological seminaries is that it is not enough just to be an evangelist and Bible student. A pastor must also be knowledgeable in the philosophy and psychology of the people to whom he ministers.

As a Christian leader he must be interested not only in "converting the lost souls"—but also in building their faith and life and applying their faith to society. That means, of course, offering instruction in the Bible. But far more than Bible knowledge should be offered. A knowledge of Christian history "after the book of Acts until our own time" is important too! Also courses in Systematic Theology as well as Biblical Theology!

So the minister's role is to be more than an evangelist. He is to be the builder and chief architect of a church. And the true Church is the body of Christ!

The pattern   The metaphor of the body of Christ is our pattern for shaping, molding and organizing the local church. A statue isn't a living body. It only looks real! So it is that many large assemblies only "look like real churches."

How do you turn a statue into a live human being? By putting into its hollow shell three systems: the blood vessels, the skeleton and the nerves.

How do you turn a "crowd gathered to hear a great preacher" or "a great crowd gathered in an evangelism tent"—how do you turn these "statues" into "true bodies"? By checking all three "systems"!

The body   The blood circulatory system of the church is evangelism. But first, we require a body to put it in. After the first six years of working in this community, I succeeded in securing land for a church site. Next we com-

62

pleted arrangements with an architect for a walk-in, drive-in church. Then, between 1955 when we held our first service of worship and 1961, we managed to build a congregation of nearly one thousand members, raise the money for and erect a magnificent structure seating that many people.

The circulatory system

Phase One was completed: the basic body was shaped and sculptured. We were now ready for Phase Two: to put in the system of blood vessels. So, the first person we added to our staff was the Minister of Evangelism. His job description was and is today: "To recruit, train and motivate laymen and laywomen to be lay evangelists of the church." And my assignment to this man was "to think in terms of adding people to the membership of the church and know that you are succeeding as long as people who have not been active members of any other church are being won into a lively membership of this church! You are, on the other hand, failing when the only people who join this church are Christians transferring from other churches."

To this minister I said, "If you really recruit and inspire and cultivate the lay people to do the job, we will have so many persons accepting Christ and joining this church that you will be kept busy the year around conducting classes, training new Christians and new potential converts in the faith and work of the church."

And my words came true. We have been adding an average of 700 members a year, two-thirds of whom were not active church members elsewhere!

As senior pastor, it is my job to *attract non-churched people into the sanctuary on Sunday mornings* through sermons *that do not sound like sermons,* but which sound like helpful and inspiring messages. Hopefully, I will lead them to an awareness of a faith in God and a faith in Jesus

Christ which is the only means of joy-filled living.

I make a strong personal appeal for commitment. And I use all the powers of persuasion that God has given me to inspire people to join the pastor's classes. Here, in a controlled classroom situation, our Minister of Evangelism and his associates are able to lead people step by step to a knowledge of the faith that saves in life and in eternity. These pastor's classes are conducted one right after another all year around, including the summer. We always start a new class in July. (Summer slumps result from summer-slumpy thinking!)

So a great church is a church that has a healthy blood supply system: new blood must be constantly generated in the form of new lives that are continually being transformed by an act of Christ. A church where Christ is at work reaching into human hearts is a living church. Unless there is a steady flow of new blood in the form of new conversions, the church will degenerate into a comfortable club. That is the beginning of a dying institution.

The skeleton

But to have a large building filled with great crowds of people, and to have them converted to the Christian faith, is still not a great church. A skeletal system, as well as a blood circulatory system, is required. Converted people must become educated Christians. If evangelism provides the blood vessel network in the body of Christ, then education is required to furnish the skeletal structure.

The second staff man added to our church was the Minister of Education. His job was and is "to recruit, train and motivate lay people to be the teachers in the church." As he began work, I told him that it would probably take five years to organize an effective educational program in the church.

The prediction proved to be accurate. When we celebrated our fifteenth anniversary in 1970, he was able to report that we had more than 300 church school teachers and youth sponsors in active service.

So far, nearly 1000 adults have received thorough Bible instruction in our training program. We believe an *inspired* congregation must also be an *informed* congregation. An intelligent body is a body that has backbone and can stand up against alien ideologies and theologies.

In keeping with the training and tradition I inherited from the perspective of the theological seminary—I believe that a program of Christian education demands more than Bible knowledge. Early in my ministry I was impressed by spokesmen and writers who talked about the "church of the laity." I observed, however, that none of these nationally renowned writers and theorists offered a program to really train the laity.

In a lecture I delivered early in my ministry I said, "The problem with the church is we do not take the training of the laity seriously." The proof of this is the lack of material to teach laymen and laywomen on how they can become the "ministers in residence" in the local church. Further proof of our historic lack of interest in training the laity to *be the ministers* is seen in the absence of a national institution that would have arisen had we really been serious about this job of turning out educated lay leaders. The American Association of Theological Schools is an institution that—if nothing else—is a monument to the seriousness with which denominations viewed the training of the clergy.

I outlined, therefore, to our Minister of Education a plan to organize in our church a "theological seminary for the laity." It would, like classical theological seminaries, offer courses in Bible, Church History, Theology, Philosophy, Psychology, Comparative Religions, as well as courses in Practical Theology, i.e., counseling, witnessing, teaching, etc.

Rev. Kenneth Van Wyk, our first Minister of Education, caught the vision and organized what may well be the first "seminary for the laity" to offer such a full range of classes. We call this lay training organization C.A.L.L. or Center for Advanced Lay Leadership. The faculty is drawn from across Southern California. Our local goal is to have no less than 1,000 trained lay persons. We require 220 units for full qualification.

And so we are building the skeleton! My greater dream is that this concept will spread until we see in America such centers for lay training across the country under a standard-setting institution like an "American Association of Accredited Lay Training Centers." I have been talking about it for twenty years and am pleased to hear the idea being discussed more and more!

Now add the nervous system. After acquiring property and buildings, after adding a Minister of Evangelism to build the membership and after adding a Minister of Education to train these members, we were now ready to add a minister to care for the daily needs and hurts of these members of its body! So we added the Minister of Family and Parish Life. This is the nervous system! *The nervous system*

As the mind can be occupied with lofty thoughts—only to have a pinprick in the finger divert the attention of the entire brain to the minor wound, so a large church must be so sensitively organized with caring and concerned lay people that no lonely member can remain unattended in a moment of pain. So our Minister of Parish life was challenged with the job description: "to *recruit, train,* and *motivate* the laymen and laywomen to do the pastoral work in this growing body."

Today, our Minister of Family and Parish Life has divided the congregation into geographical zones of eight families each. A lay pastor watches over the seven families in his geographic zone. Eight zones in a geographic area form a division with another lay pastor serving as the division leader. In this way, the large congregation is organized with lay people trained to shepherd, care for and pastor the membership.

The nervous system is beautifully supplemented in Garden Grove Community Church by dozens of sharing and caring groups. I'll let one of the small group leaders from our church describe this exciting ministry:

"Brothers and sisters in Christ are practicing love and compassion on one another first, before extending it to the world around them. Each family fellowship group has a unique personality and is made up of individuals in varying degrees of spiritual growth. Sometimes the group succeeds and sometimes it fails, both individually and together, but with God's help they keep working together. At each meeting there is prayer, Scripture, a quiet time and a sharing time. The blessings that come from such sharing times are many:

We are learning how to lose ourselves in others.

"By freeing ourselves from spiritual problems and by gaining a healthy love and respect for ourselves, we are becoming liberated. Getting ourselves off our hands frees us to lend a helping hand to others, and every time this happens in a group, we call it a modern-day miracle.

We are learning how to listen deeply.

"Too often conversations become monologues rather than dialogues. Too often we 'tune in' and 'tune out' at random. But in a small sharing group, everyone in the circle gets his turn to talk. The shy one no longer has to fight the aggressive talker. Everyone listens as each person takes his turn. Shy, frightened persons learn how to open up and reveal themselves as they grow in trust.

"We learn to hear the silent words of the soul as well as the spoken words of the lips. Persons who have never prayed aloud learn to utter their first child-like petitions to God. Every time this happens in a group, our eyes are wet with joy.

We are learning how to love the unlovely.

"Since no two people are exactly alike, each group is made up of a variety of different individuals, some with peculiar idiosyncrasies that one might ordinarily walk away from. But in small groups, we stick it out if we wish to stay in the group, and eventually we learn how to unlock the hidden blessings in the person we judged as unlovely. We learn to accept people just as they are—as God was willing to do with us when we first came to him.

We are learning how to leave our mistakes at the foot of the cross.

"Confession and reconciliation are good for the soul. Freed from guilt through forgiveness, we can proceed with God's next assignment rather than waste needless energy on unrepented mistakes. Praying companions make this easier and remind us when we tend to forget.

We are learning how to discover God's plan for our lives.

"Through searching the Scriptures and by sharing collective insights and actual experiences, God can reveal to His modern-day disciples His step-by-step plan for our lives. One man feels led to change jobs; another feels challenged to stay where he is. One couple feels led to get involved with teen-agers, others to start a blood bank, adopt children, take in foster children, help welfare families, repair missionary machinery in Mexico, provide clothing for an orphanage, counsel persons in need through phone calls or through letters received from our television and radio outreach, or volunteer their services in various programs and activities within the local church.

We are learning how to lean on the power of the Holy Spirit.

"The third Person of the Trinity is no stranger to the people in small sharing groups. We have learned to depend on His supernatural power during the traumatic or everyday experiences of life. Accidents, alcoholism, blindness, bankruptcy, cancer, death, divorce, drug addiction, heart attacks, mental illness, runaways, suicide and unemployment have all been experienced and lived through by real people surrounded by real, live fellowship groups — undergirded by the power of the Spirit working in and through people.

We are learning to lead others to Christ.

"Each member of a group makes reports to his group every two weeks, telling of his day-to-day encounters with God — God's assignments, His corrections, His blessings, His guidance, and His revelations. Talking about Christ becomes so natural and so easy. It finally becomes second nature to share these vital experiences with unchurched neighbors. This often helps to open the door of their hearts so that Christ can come in.

"Small groups are certainly one way to The Way. They help us, the human body of Christ, become more deeply aware of the Body's many parts — hurting when others hurt, rejoicing when others rejoice, lifting when others are down, supporting when others are weak, loving when others are discouraged.

"It works! Garden Grove has tried it and has seen it work!"[1]

It is the goal of the Garden Grove Community Church to have a membership made up of persons won through evangelism and whose lives have been changed through the life-giving power of Christ. They will have been educated through our adult education program, and they will be held together as one caring, sharing and loving community by the nervous system of our church.

Eventually one thousand lay pastors, all graduates of the Center for Advanced Lay Leadership, will shepherd this great congregation! We have not reached that goal yet! I hope to reach it when we celebrate our twenty-fifth birthday as a church. Then, and only then, will Garden Grove Community Church be, in my mind, a truly great church!

Your church in your community may not have the potential for a large membership, but your church must have the blood circulatory system of evangelism, the skeletal system of education and the nervous system of trained laity caring for its fellow citizens in Christ, if your church is to be a true Church: a body of Christ leading, loving and lifting your community.

And the church that is truly the body of Chris is the kind of an institution that will never be out-of-date! It is the kind of a church that will be as modern as the Twenty-First Century!

Footnotes

1. Mary Lee Ehrlich, "Modern-Day Disciples," *The Church Herald*, Garden Grove Community Church, October 22, 1971), pp. 12,13.

71

Chapter 8

Setting Goals
for Outstanding
Success

Lack of goal
setting

Set successful goals and you will succeed. Fail to set successful goals and you can be assured of failure.

Success or failure starts at this point, for goal setting is nothing more than planning ahead. And when you fail to plan, you plan to fail. Putting it another way, *when you set no goals for growth, you set your goals for no growth!*

The terrible truth is that tens of thousands of churches around the world today are experiencing no growth simply because nobody established any growth goal. I have talked to pastors of churches in Hong Kong, Japan, India, Korea, Greece, Europe, the Middle East and America. I have read hundreds of Self-Study Guides of ministers and church leaders who enter our Institute for Successful Leadership. And I can report that few pastors and few churches have set any firm, clear-cut goals for growth.

Now this is an unforgivable sin for a person who is supposedly a leader in the movement which is commissioned to go "into all the world, and preach the gospel to every creature" (Mark 16:15).

What are the reasons for this lack of goal setting?

Perhaps the biggest single reason is that the typical pastor comes to the church *without the determination to stay there long enough to make it a great church.* I have done enough private counseling with ministers of all denominations to report that the majority of ministers accept the call or assignment to a church with the expectation of staying on only until something better comes along.

Transiency of pastors

Others look upon the church that is financially self-supporting as a "success." They see their goal as nothing more than "greasing the machinery" and keeping the machine going. Obviously, such an attitude is not going to produce a dynamic evangelistic spirit which will produce the new blood which keeps the church lively and exciting.

I am certain Garden Grove Community Church would not be the church it is today if I had not been deeply impressed earlier in my life by two persons. One of these, as I previously mentioned, was Dr. Raymond Lindquist, of First Presbyterian Church, Hollywood, California, who challenged us never to take a church "unless you can envision spending your life there."

At this same time I was asked to write a term paper on George Truett. When the assignment was given to me, I hadn't the faintest idea who he was. But I soon found out, and I've never forgotten it.

George Truett accepted a call to a small Baptist church in Dallas, Texas. He took the long look and envisioned spending his life there. And he did! He devoted more than forty years of his life to this congregation. As a result, he was able to think long thoughts, plan great dreams and set enormous goals. It is no wonder that, when his ministry was terminated, he left behind the largest Baptist church—and perhaps the greatest Baptist church—in America. The real proof of the success of his ministry lies in the fact that now, many years after he has gone, the church continues to grow in a vital and dynamic way.

So it was, through the comment by Dr. Lindquist and the inspiration of Dr. Truett, God gave me the desire to find a church where I could devote my entire lifetime.

Fear of failure   Another major reason for lack of goal-setting by church leaders is *the fear of failure*. When I had established a clear mental picture of the walk-in, drive-in church that I hoped to build, complete with fountains, landscaping and tower, I was a very excited young man. Remember, goal-setting is a major source of enthusiasm—and enthusiasm is all-important for success.

I did not dare at first to reveal my dream publicly. I had a dream, you see, but it was not yet a goal. Why not? Because I kept it a secret, and only dreams that are publicly announced become goals.

I was afraid that if I announced my dream and accepted it as a goal to be sought, I would run the risk of failure. And the fear of failure, perhaps more than any other single factor, is the reason why the average human being does not establish challenging goals for himself.

Let me tell you what cured me of my fear of failure. I was visiting an eastern church on a preaching assignment. There, in that great church, I saw a calendar with this slogan written across the top of that particular month: "I'd rather attempt to do something great and fail than attempt to do nothing and succeed."

That did it! I suddenly realized that "not failure but low aim is crime." Since then, I have never been afraid of publicly establishing and announcing great goals.

74

Overcome your fear of failure. As one of my books states, there are seven ways you can do so.[1] I do not believe that God will ever scold you for having attempted to dare something for Him. But I do believe that some of us will stand before God someday and be accused of having had too little faith.

Still another reason why people resist setting goals is *their own lack of self-confidence*. At this point I urge you to read most carefully my other book, *Move Ahead with Possibility Thinking*.[2] You can accomplish anything you can imagine, providing your goals meet certain principles. You can, in fact, test the success potential of your goals before you actually launch them. If your goals meet the following criteria, they will succeed—if you only have enough nerve to announce them, begin them and never give up.

Lack of self-confidence

Test your goals in this way: ask these three questions to determine whether your goals are wise and attainable.

Test your goals

Is this a problem-solving goal?

Does this goal—this dream—solve human problems? This is the test of practicality.

The terrible thing is that most people begin by asking the question: "Can I afford it? Do we have the money?" This is the last question to be asked.

The first questions must always be: "Would this be a great thing for God? Would it be a great thing for Jesus Christ? Would it be a great thing for our community? Would it help a lot of human beings? Would it solve a lot of human problems? Is anybody else doing the job right?"

If your goals would help to solve human problems, move ahead to the next question.

Can this dream, my glorified goal, be pacesetting?

Obviously, if another church or several churches in your community are already succeeding in doing what you hope to do, then you can expect some rough competition. I was enormously encouraged to build our walk-in, drive-in church and was confident of success because this was the only walk-in, drive-in church in all of Orange County. I have said that we have succeeded, not because we are so smart, but because the competition just didn't exist!

If your glorified goal, your exciting dream, is pacesetting, you can be assured of enormous publicity. As a result, the people who stand to benefit by your services will know you're in business! And this is all-important—for people must get behind any goal to make it succeed. No man is an island. Even the artist who works completely alone on a canvas needs customers to buy his paintings or he will starve.

If your goal passes the first and second questions, then move on to the third question.

Can this goal be exciting—really exciting—to people?

Obviously, if it fails to excite people, they will not get behind the project. And people will get excited about goals if they see that these goals are really practical—and if they will help human beings who are hurting. People will get excited about goals if they see that these goals can be creative and can lead to something beautiful.

I tell the members of my staff that I will listen to any suggestion if it has a superlative in it. If it is the "first" or

76

the "longest" or the "shortest" or "newest" or "oldest." If it excels, it will attract attention because it is an award winner, then I know that it has excitement-generating potential and will become relatively easy to sell.

The goal of a walk-in, drive-in church was established firmly in my mind as a guaranteed successful idea because it passed the above three questions. People who are physically handicapped, or have mentally retarded children, or want to avoid crowds, or are mourning and given to crying in a sanctuary, or wish to maintain their privacy—these are some of the people with problems who are benefited by a drive-in church. Obviously, a walk-in, drive-in church could solve human problems.

Furthermore, there was nothing like it in the United States, or for that matter in the entire world, so it was pacesetting. I could be assured that I would get the attention of many people. And I would need the attention of many people in order to attract the support that would make success possible.

Beauty is practical as well as desirable! That's why I could envision the walk-in, drive-in church being designed so attractively, so beautifully, that people would be magnetically drawn to it. People run away from ugliness; people run to beauty. Beauty excites. Beauty generates enthusiasm. Beauty marshals enormous support. I envisioned reflecting pools, fountains, green grass with splashes of flower gardens. I envisioned award-winning, futuristic architecture. *Beauty as a goal*

So test your dreams by the above questions and begin now to set growth goals for your church. But how do you begin? First, *determine what the unchurched population* *Set membership goals*

77

of your community is today, what it will be ten years from today, twenty years from today and fifty years from today. Your local chamber of commerce will have studies that will give you the answers.

Then ask yourself this question: "What percentage of the unchurched population from our community could we win into our membership if we had a tremendous staff, marvelous facilities including surplus parking, and a program for all ages?" In arriving at your answers, you can assume that people will drive as far as twenty miles one way if you are near a major freeway. Or most people will be willing to drive twenty minutes to a church that has the goods!

For myself, I find that twenty minutes, or twenty miles, or ten stop lights is the limit of my tolerance. And I believe that this applies to many people in our modern society. In arriving at the population of your potential parish zone, draw a radius of twenty minutes' driving distance, or ten miles if there are several stop signs or stop lights.

Perhaps you should establish a goal of canvassing door-to-door, all of the homes in your community. Then actually *draw up a mailing list of all of the non-churched people* in your territory. When you have done this, you will know more realistically what the prospects for your church membership growth will be. Do not assume that thousands of homes are too many to canvass.

In the early days of our church, when we had less than 200 members, we canvassed 14,000 homes in only two weeks. It can be done very simply. All we did was have one person ride down every street while his wife drove the car. He wrote down the name of the street and the number of every house. Forty addresses appeared on a sheet of paper from the top to the bottom. And so a total of 350 sheets with 40 addresses on a sheet amounted to 14,000 addresses.

We recruited thirty-five teams of persons and gave to

each team ten sheets with forty addresses — or 400 calls to make. They did this in two Saturdays. They simply went from house to house and asked one brief question: "Are you an active member of a local church?" If the answer was "no" they made a simple check mark on the sheet, left an invitational brochure and moved on. The names and addresses of all the unchurched people were placed on a stenciled mailing list and we had the beginnings of a tremendous field that we could work!

No matter how small your church is, you must begin by setting membership growth goals. If you have a very small church, you can begin by keeping on your desk a list of all of the prospective members of your church. I did this for years. If you don't have a prospect list on your desk, then go out and call from door to door to build a prospect list! *And begin by working the prospect list.*

Then establish quarterly goals to win people to Jesus Christ. Really, the secret of winning people to Christ and into a growing membership of the church is so very simple! Success starts when you start to set goals!

How large should a church ultimately be? *The answer to that question must be based on the unchurched population of your community.* Calculate what percentage of the unchurched you can reasonably expect to win in the next twenty or thirty years, and let this determine your ultimate membership goal. The ultimate potential membership of your church, based upon prayerful expectations of the maximum number of unchurched people you can win to Christ out of your large community in the next thirty years, should be the *only* basis upon which your membership goals are established.

I cannot urge too strongly that word, ONLY! No other criterion should determine your membership goals. Not the theories of some writer. Nor the ideas of some "management consultant." Nor the seating capacity of your sanctuary. Nor the size of your parking lot! One factor and one factor only sets the membership growth goals. And that is *the number of unchurched people in your community!*

Now that you've set membership goals, establish church attendance goals. Up that goal! If your sanctuary is almost filled, plan two services. Let your goal be to fill the church twice. When you force yourself to establish these church attendance goals, you will be forced to think of possible ways to raise the attendance. This will force you to think in terms of better programming, better public relations, better advertising and more aggressive door-to-door calling. Up that church attendance goal right now!

Now begin to work on program goals! And how do you establish goals for programs? You might find yourself stimulated by reading material that comes from your denominational headquarters.

But let me give you a very practical assignment that is the best advice anyone will ever give to you on establishing program goals for a successful, growing church in your community:

Have your secretary (if you don't have a secretary, you'd better get out and make your church grow large enough so you can afford one!) block off two weeks in your calendar when you will attend no committee meetings, accept no public assignments, and perhaps have your board bring in two guest ministers for two Sundays.

Allocate these two weeks *full time* toward the following project: begin by calling door-to-door in the immediate vicinity of your church. You have called on some of these homes before, but you are going to call now with a different purpose, a different motive, and a different question.

You are going to ask: "Do you attend our church regularly? Have you ever attended it? Do you attend any other church?"

If they give you a negative answer, you will reply by saying: "I'm delighted to hear this because I'm anxious to find out how I can improve this church and make it such an exciting church that intelligent and wonderful people like you will want to come. You are obviously an intelligent person, so you undoubtedly have good reasons why you don't attend the church. Would you please tell me what they are? And could you tell me what our church could possibly do to help in any area of your life? Is there any program that you would be interested in?"

Generally, after you have asked the first one or two questions, the answers will be forthcoming. I did this years ago and it was an eye-opening experience! I heard criticisms of "typical sermons." And I heard criticisms about other gaps in the church program. The criticisms of the unchurched persons in my community became a major learning experience!

If you will spend two weeks calling door-to-door in an ever-widening circle, beginning from your church property, and will listen with an open mind, then indeed you will have the education of a lifetime! Listen to the individuals you talk with—listen to them carefully.

Do not be defensive! In spite of all that you have ever been taught, assume—for one humble time in your life—that you may have been wrong about a lot of things! So, listen to what the unchurched are saying and you will find out where they are hurting, where they are frightened, where they are worried. Take careful notes. Keep a daily diary detailing your calls.

After two weeks you will know what kind of a church program you have to design to meet the needs of these people in your community. You will know what kind of messages to give in order to bring them into the church.

Not only will you be enlightened, but you will be mentally and socially prepared to establish program and sermon goals. You will even discover what kind of staff members should be added to your church.

Set new goals   Never allow anything to keep you from setting new goals once the old goals have been attained. Where there are no goals — then and there the seeds of death are sown. The dullest, deadest and most unpleasant time in my life came when, after fourteen years in the Garden Grove Community Church, I found my forty years' goals accomplished!

Victor Frankl said in a lecture once: "The *is* must never catch up with the *ought*." When the Israelites traveled across the wilderness, they never caught up with the cloud by day or with the fire by night. There must always be the tension between the unreached goal and the present state of affairs. When there are no challenging goals, then death has already set in.

If anything blocks the way to establishing larger and more challenging goals, then by all means remove these obstacles to growth goals! Growth-restricting barriers must be removed at any cost or the seed of death is planted. Our original church property was ten acres in size. This allowed for 700 parking spaces off the street. When the parking lot was filled twice on Sunday morning, I could see cars drive in and out and storm away because they could find no parking space.

We had a growth-restricting problem. Either we would create more parking or growth goals would be unattainable. At a price of one million dollars, we removed the problem of inadequate parking. We bought ten acres of land next door. It was one of the smartest things we ever did in the history of our church!

When our sanctuary was enlarged to its maximum

82

seating capacity of 1700, and when it was filled to over-flowing in two morning church services, we had another growth-restricting problem which threatened the realization of our goals in increased membership. As a result, we determined to solve this growth-restricting, goal-frustrating problem at any cost. We were prepared, if necessary, to destroy the entire sanctuary to build a larger one if need be.

It would be a sin, we felt, to allow a building made out of glass and steel and aluminum to frustrate the winning of more people to Jesus Christ! We would not surrender leadership to a chunk of real estate. So we solved the problem by announcing three morning church services and I began preaching at 8:30, again at 10:00, and again at 11:15 A.M.

As this book goes to press I am in the process of raising $4 million to build a larger sanctuary seating four thousand persons. Why? Because there are still over 500,000 unchurched people in a 15-minute radius of our church! We have an idea how many unchurched people we can win in our community! On that basis we *need* a sanctuary seating four thousand to hold them all!

Other than our commission from Christ, *the challenge of the unchurched people — more than anything else — sets the goals in our church.* And if that should ever change you will see Garden Grove Community Church begin to die.

By all means, set goals *beyond* your goals. And if there are any obstacles in the way that would keep you from establishishing larger goals, realize that these obstacles must be removed at any cost — or accept the fact that the seed of death and decay is already planted. If you can't afford to pay the price of removing your growth-stifling obstacles, then be prepared to pay the price of ''not being

Set goals beyond goals

83

able to afford it"—and that price tag is *death!*

What this means is that you must become a possibility thinker to succeed! In setting your goals, believe that anything is possible if it can solve human problems and if it can be a great thing for God.

Use possibility thinking to set your goals. And now use possibility thinking to dream up all of the possible ways to reach what may seem now to be an impossible goal!

Footnotes

1. Robert H. Schuller, *Self-Love: The Dynamic Force of Success* (New York: Hawthorn Books, Inc., 1969).
2. Robert H. Schuller, *Move Ahead with Possibility Thinking* (New York: Doubleday & Company, 1967).

Chapter 9

Possibility Thinking Makes Miracles Happen

The greatest power in the world is the power of possibility thinking. If your dream has come from God then you need only to exercise this miracle-working power, and you can reach the seemingly unattainable goal! Believe me, I know!

All right, your goals are already firmly established in your mind. And they have successfully passed the three-way question test. So far, so good. But now at this point, your biggest problem is you. Yes, you! The hardest job before you now is to make yourself believe that the apparently enormous goal is somehow, some way, somewhere, sometime attainable.

But you can do it, unless you are a victim of impossibility thinking. Yes, only you can make the possible goal impossible. How?

Impossibility thinking

85

You make a possible goal impossible when you do nothing about it. You make a possible goal impossible when you quit somewhere along the way. You make a possible goal impossible when you accept failure as final.

So what then is possibility thinking?

Possibility thinking is the maximum utilization of the God-given powers of imagination exercised in dreaming up possible ways by which a desired objective can be attained. Possibility thinking is also called faith, the kind of faith Jesus Christ was talking about when He said, "If you have faith as a grain of mustard seed, you will say to this mountain, 'Move . . . ,' and it will move; and nothing will be impossible to you" (Matt. 17:20, *RSV*).

The principles of possibility thinking are these:

Possibility thinking assumes that there must be a way to achieve a desired objective.

This is so when it is established that that same objective would be a great thing for God, a tremendous thing for Jesus Christ and a problem-solving means for helping many hurting human beings.

Possibility thinking makes great pronouncements.

In this way you reveal to the public your sincere intention to accomplish this exciting and most necessary objective.

Possibility thinking results in brainstorming.

Motivated by the assumption of achievement and committed by public pronouncement, possibility thinkers begin to brainstorm. And in brainstorming, an amazing assortment of creative ideas will be forthcoming—ideas which will unlock possible ways to success that you would never have thought of at all, if you had not exercised possibility thinking in the first place!

Possibility thinking brings in support from unexpected sources.

The positive idea let loose will be grabbed hold of by people who will become the followers of the idea and will not let it die. At this point, the goal is already halfway attained!

Never say "No!"

I have adopted a policy never to make a "no" decision on a potentially good idea. If any idea is ever suggested to my mind by God, or by a fellow mortal, I—by an act of sheer will power—refuse to make a negative response. I intuitively test proposals by the three success-spotting questions and, if I get the right answers, I move ahead and *assume* that the objective can be accomplished. If it is not God's will for success to be forthcoming, I will let Him make the "no" decision! There are a million ways in which God can stop us!

God is unlimited

And God has unlimited financial resources and unlimited intelligence to achieve His goals. *Possibility thinking is simply opening your mind for God to unfold the ways in which His will can be accomplished.* Thus God performs miracles in the people who, unafraid of failure and public embarrassment, move boldly and bravely forward attempting big things for God and expecting great things from God.

87

Nothing is impossible   At this point, let me share three never-to-be-forgotten experiences that I have gone through since I published the book on possibility thinking some years ago.

Our original walk-in, drive-in sanctuary was built on ten acres of land which we purchased at a total cost of $66,000, or $6600 per acre. At that time, we tried to buy an additional ten acres of adjoining land, anticipating a future need. We offered the owner $12,000 an acre, an unheard of amount! The offer was refused. Later, we offered him $25,000 an acre—a quarter of a million dollars! Again the offer was turned down.

Many years later, we offered him $50,000 an acre, or a half-million dollars! And believe me, this took an enormous amount of possibility thinking to offer $500,000 for the same amount of ground that we had bought only a few years earlier for $66,000! Once again our offer was refused.

A few months after this last offer was rejected, a huge development combine came in, purchased 200 acres directly across the street from our church, and took out a lease-option on the adjoining ten acres that we had bid for unsuccessfully. The lease they secured on the land was for five years, with an option to buy the acreage at the end of that period for $500,000. When I discovered that we had lost out, I accepted defeat. "We'll never get it now," I thought to myself.

In spite of the apparent setback, we proceeded to enlarge our sanctuary from its original seating capacity of 1000 to its master-plan size designed to accommodate 1700 persons. We proceeded to erect the Tower of Hope, a 14-story structure housing the 24-hour telephone counseling services in the chapel at the top, offices for the growing staff, counseling clinic and classrooms. By now the added stimulus of the additional building projects created so much publicity and attention in the community that attendance soared.

88

Twelve months after we enlarged our sanctuary, we found ourselves with a parking problem. I had now moved into my office on the twelfth floor of the Tower. From this vantage point I could see what was going on in the parking lot and in the adjoining streets.

I realize now that, if we had not built the Tower, and if my office had remained in its former cloistered, paneled seclusion of the garden setting, our church would not have grown as it has today, for I would not have been aware of the parking and traffic problem. But when I was elevated high in the sky and looked down on the congestion on the streets and the futility of cars driving in and out looking for a place to park, I became deeply aware of the fact that our success was about to strangle us.

Addressing the church board, I made the following comment, ''Growth will lift you or it will level you. It can propel you forward or it can knock you down and grind you into the ground. Look at the old downtown sections in this country.

''The original merchants were so swamped with new customers when the first suburbs were built that they were confident of continued success. They were not, however, sustained by growth for long. Soon they found that they were incapable of handling the crowds. Parking became impossible.

''So, enterprising merchants began building great new shopping centers on the outskirts of the old towns. The result? With the new shopping centers in business, the old downtown merchants died—strangled by growth.''

It became clear to us that we would have to obtain additional parking. There were only two possible ways in which this desired goal could be accomplished: either buy more land or build a high-rise parking garage on our present land.

First, we investigated the possibilities of the high-rise garage with its racks or elevators lifting cars to the second, third and fourth stories. Our findings indicated that it would cost approximately five dollars per square foot. At the same time, it would necessarily be a huge structure creating an undesirable visual intrusion into the spacious atmosphere of the 10-acre property.

Suddenly our thinking had been enormously stretched, and the biggest job in the world is to think bigger than you've ever thought before! So, we made a new approach to the syndicate that held the lease-option on the adjoining ten acres. We were prepared to offer more than $50,000 an acre, which was their option.

Upon approaching them, however, we were informed that the property was not for sale at any price. We prayed. We practiced possibility thinking and believed that somehow it might be possible to acquire the land. About that time, I called our banker and he told me, "Did you hear the news? Edgar Kaiser has taken over control of the combine that owns the property around your place."

I prayed and suddenly I remembered reading, some twenty years before, a lead article in the *Reader's Digest* which was a condensation of the layman's sermon preached by Henry J. Kaiser at New York's Marble Collegiate Church where Dr. Norman Vincent Peale is the pastor. I immediately called my friend Norman Vincent Peale and asked him, "Do you know Edgar Kaiser?" He replied that he knew Mr. Kaiser very well. At my request Dr. Peale appealed to Mr. Kaiser to sell us their "option." Within forty-eight hours, I received a call from Charles Cobb, Kaiser's man in control, inviting me to come in and negotiate for the property!

It was then the middle of February of 1969. The business administrator and I met with Mr. Cobb who told us that the property, on the advice of Mr. Kaiser, could be made available to us. The price would be $135,000 an acre, or $1,350,000! Now, by all human rationale, that figure was out of our reach. We countered with an offer of $1,000,000.

Mr. Cobb subsequently agreed to sell the property to us for that sum, "Providing," he said, "that I can get $500,000 cash for our position by March 31"—just six weeks away. He explained that the payment was needed to get his firm's apartment project off the ground ahead of schedule. This, he said, would generate increased income by the apartment project, justifying the lower sale price.

I called a church board meeting and appraised them of the facts. "For the first time in our history—and for the only time—you have an opportunity to buy the adjoining ten acres of ground. It is an opportunity that has never come before and that will never come again if you turn it down today. We can buy the property for $1,000,000. That's about $2.50 a square foot—half the price the parking structure will cost and you get full frontage rights and all air rights! It's a bargain! The only thing is, we have to come up with $500,000 in cold, hard cash in the next forty-five days."

The board passed the following resolution: "To give God a chance to work a miracle, we would have Dr. Schuller announce on the coming Sunday our intention to raise this amount of money and buy the property." The resolution passed without a dissenting vote, and the next Sunday we made the announcement to the congregation.

Now you know, no conventional fund raiser is going to come in and attempt to conduct and wrap up a campaign from beginning to end in six short weeks. It just can't be done—or so they say. So I called in a friend of mine who operates a professional fund-raising organization and we hired him to recruit and train members of our church for an accelerated money-raising campaign.

And we did it! It was the most concentrated, most urgent appeal for financial help we've ever made in the history of our church.

91

As soon as we announced publicly our intention to buy the property, I received a phone call from the banker of our church who asked: "What are you doing?"

We told him.

Without hesitation, he replied by saying, "I think it's a great idea! If we can help you out, we'd like to do so. In fact, if you people can actually collect $250,000 in cash in the next six weeks, we will loan you the other $250,000 for a period of twenty-four months."

This was great news! Now it meant that all we'd have to collect from the congregation during those forty-five days was $250,000. Time passed with amazing swiftness as the campaign progressed — much too rapidly. Just three days before the payment deadline, we found that we had only $160,000 on hand!

Suddenly the phone rang. It was the lawyer from the Kaiser group. "You know," he said, "we aren't going to be able to finish the legal work before March 31. There are some signatures we need from some of our people who are out of the area. Is it all right if we extend the agreement for another three weeks?"

"I will have to discuss it with my advisors," I replied.

Then after a very short pause, I said, "Oh, that will be great! That will be just fine with us!"

By the third week of April 1969 we had the required $250,000 and had also borrowed $250,000 from the bank. The $500,000 was deposited and we took over the option to buy the ten acres from the original owner for $500,000. After all the legal papers had been signed, our treasurer, Frank Boss, and I went back to our office jubilantly carrying the legal document, which was about three-quarters of an inch thick!

Then we began wrestling with the next problem. Where were we going to obtain the remaining $500,000 to complete the purchase in July? Imagine our happy surprise when we opened the document and read the fine print. In addition to verifying the fact that we had the right to purchase the land with a down payment of $500,000 in July, the document specified: "This price offer will hold firm for the next five years."

At that time, if we elected to exercise the option and actually purchase the property for $500,000, it would be sold to us on the following terms: $100,000 down, with ten years to pay off the balance at six percent interest. And *so a million-dollar financial package fell together in less than two months time!*

Today that property is developed and our parking has been increased by 700 cars. A new youth center stands in the corner of the new property and we have a marvelous plan for our larger new sanctuary on that land.

Without any doubt, the addition of that property kept our church from dying! And it opened up a fantastic future for us! We now have twenty acres at the freeway hub of Orange County. And it all became possible simply because we got out of God's way, assuming and believing that when we get out of His way, *God specializes in turning impossibilities into possibilities!*

Only five months after this enormously aggressive and successful fund-raising program, I made the acquaintance of Fred Dinert. Fred and I were chatting in my office about the prospects for a television ministry emanating from the Garden Grove Community Church. I could envision a most spectacular color telecast of our church services. We do have a phenomenal natural setting, with trees, flowers and fountains lending a spirit of beauty and serenity to the church grounds.

Fred and I discussed the possibility of an hour-long television color program and he agreed to give me an estimate as to the cost. He came back with this report: "It can be done, Bob, but it will cost around $400,000 a year."

I replied with this impossibility statement: "We can

93

never do that. Certainly, we couldn't do it today. Perhaps in four years we could. But at this point in time it would be impossible to try to raise any extra money from our people who have just been hit for all the money we could get out of them."

Then, like a real impossibility thinker, I added, "Furthermore, in November—only a few weeks from now —we'll be asking them to underwrite the next year's budget which is going to be increased over this year's by $100,000! So I suppose we'll simply have to forget the televising idea at this time."

Well, Fred Dinert called me a few weeks later. "Bob, I think you should let God decide whether it is possible. Why don't you and I give God a chance to make this decision. *If the decision is no, let God make it.* Next Sunday have your people come to church and lay the plan before them. Let them respond.

"You and I and your business administrator, Frank Boss, will make a quiet prayer covenant with God. We will tell God to show us $200,000 worth of support in two weeks time, if He wants this television ministry to begin. If we can receive pledges in that amount, we will go on the air in January and trust that the balance of the money will come in the next twelve or twenty-four months."

So Fred Dinert, in Philadelphia, and Frank Boss and Bob Schuller in Garden Grove made this quiet prayer covenant with God.

On the following Sunday, the people came to church after being notified in advance that "Dr. Schuller was about to make one of the most important decisions of his life and that he would ask the members of the congregation to direct him." Persons in attendance that Sunday morning found pledge cards in the bulletin. That morning alone, 1100 families pledged $186,000. And on the following Sunday, the pledges totaled $203,000!

God had taught me a big lesson. He taught me that I was "too-little-a-thinker"!

We proceeded to form a corporation which we called The Robert Schuller TeleVangelism Association, Incorporated. I selected the treasurer and business administrator of the church to be the treasurer of the new corporation, so that I would be personally immune from financial criticism in the handling, receiving and discharging of funds. I hired Stuart Ehrlich, a layman from the church to be my full-time administrative aide, handling the administrative detail of this new project as well as the details connected with the Institute for Successful Church Leadership, another project I was about to launch!

By the first Sunday in January, the first pledge payments came in, totaling approximately $4,000. Since we were beginning from scratch, we wanted to postpone the beginning of the telecast as deep into the year as we could in order to build up a small financial "base." So we announced to the congregation that we would videotape our first service on the third Sunday in January of 1970, and would begin actual telecasting the first Sunday in February.

It was on a Wednesday morning in the middle of January that Frank Boss came into my office with bad news. "Bob, in order to live up to our word and begin videotaping on the third Sunday in January, we are going to have to have special lights installed *tomorrow!* And here's the bad news—the lights, plus a new transformer, will come to $20,000! And to make matters worse, they demand cash on the line—no credit. All the money we have available at this point is $10,000!"

Well, I had one day's time to find the solution to the problem. Deep within myself, I couldn't condone the idea of "borrowing" from the church corporation. I knew they simply didn't have the surplus cash.

Frankly, I didn't know what to do. Furthermore, I

didn't have time to think about the problem during the course of the day because I had a heavy schedule of commitments. I decided to finish my work and then put my mind to confronting this latest crisis.

My last appointment for the day was a couple whom I had never met before. They walked into my office that Wednesday night with beaming faces. "What's your problem?" I asked. They informed that they had no problem but that they wished to discuss another matter.

The husband explained: "When we became Christians, we decided to tithe. Our business has just been fantastic ever since! When you asked for pledges in November for the television ministry, we wanted to pledge something but didn't know how much we would be able to promise.

"But now we have a report from our accountant which indicates that the profits of our business in 1969 have been so good that we are in a position to give the Lord a substantial amount, enough to bring in our full tithe. So we have a check that we would like to present to you for your television program."

They handed me the check. I took it, looked at it, and tears flowed from my eyes. It was a check for $10,000!

It was God's way of saying, "Schuller, this is My project. Stay out of My way. Only be willing to think big, believe big and pray big—and big things will happen!"

The next morning Frank Boss signed the contract with the lighting contractors. The lights were installed and the transformer was connected. And right on schedule, we videotaped our first program on the third Sunday in January! We began televising, exactly as we had promised, the first Sunday in February.

Impossibilities become possibilities   Why did these impossibilities prove, with God's leadership, to become possibilities? Both the acquisition of the extra ten acres and the television project illustrate the

96

principles of spotting success before you launch your goal.

The television program solved many problems. It filled a vital human need. It was a great thing for God and continues to be a great thing for God! People need inspiration. And in our area, there are 13 million people who live within the range of the television station over which we televise.

The second principle is also in operation here: our one-hour color television church service is pacesetting. Ours was the first Protestant church in Southern California that televised its services every Sunday. Nobody else was doing the job!

The third principle comes into play as well. Our program contains beauty and creativity. The use of our attractive setting of orange trees, fountains, sliding walls that move open, bells ringing in the Tower, and members of our congregation seated within the sanctuary, in the garden and in their cars—all are captured by the television cameras to present an excitingly attractive program which generates great enthusiasm and consequently marshals enormous support.

If the goals that you are establishing in your mind meet the three success-spotting principles—then *only you can make these goals impossible by doing nothing about them or by quitting too quickly.*

Play the game

For the most productive and exciting time of your life, pick some fantastic goal, some tremendous goal, that will pass the three success-spotting principles. Then get together with one, two or perhaps three possibility thinkers and play the possibility-thinking game!

When you start playing the game, here's what happens. The wild and reckless ideas that you have allowed to be expressed in your slumbering subconscious get stirred up.

So, wild and reckless ideas bump into some snoozing, creative brain cells that—once jarred out of their slumber—perk up and listen to what's going on. They emerge from their hibernation to join the party and offer their own suggestions.

After awhile, more sleeping, creative brain cells are aroused by all the activity and great ideas come forth until the "list of possible ways" is lengthened and, generally speaking, a more probable solution is mentally generated.

What are your goals? What are your dreams? What great thing can you imagine for God? Play the possibility-thinking game.

"If you have faith as a grain of mustard seed, you will say to this mountain, 'Move . . . ,' and it will move; and nothing will be impossible to you" (Matt. 17:20, *RSV*).

Now, be a believer. And begin by believing you can sell your ideas to your church people!

Chapter 10

How You Can Sell Your Ideas Successfully

You have determined under God to become an inspiring leader of your church. And, looking toward Century Twenty-One, you have established exciting goals for your church. You have also saturated your mind with the Christ Spirit of possibility thinking.

So how do you go about sharing and successfully selling your ideas to the people who alone can help you make those dreams come true? I can summarize my first fifteen years in the Garden Grove Community Church pulpit as time spent primarily in setting goals, testing them before God, and then selling them successfully to the people who really did it all!

And what is successful selling? It is not manipulation, it is communication! Successful selling is communicating to people a *truth* they weren't aware of before. Now follow these steps:

1

Concentrate on the "problem" your idea will solve.

If you don't have a problem the odds are you won't move ahead. To try to sell the idea of a new sanctuary if a congregation already has a fine, serviceable facility will not be easy. But let the building burn down and problem is obvious.

So test your idea: Does it really fill a vital need? Does it solve a serious problem? Does it heal a hurt?

Dramatize the problem.

Remember this: you will very likely fail in any enterprise that does not offer solutions to real and honest problems. Therefore, possibility thinking is correct when it says that every problem is an opportunity. The only reason we were able to develop the walk-in, drive-in church, internationally pacesetting as it was, was due to the fact that we had a terribly real problem!

After three years of operation, I found myself with a congregation worshiping at 9:30 on a Sunday morning, in a beautiful chapel located on a two-acre grassy suburban lot in the heart of the Garden Grove community. At 11 o'clock every Sunday morning, I found myself the pastor of our drive-in congregation meeting in a drive-in theater three miles away on the freeway. We had a major problem.

For future planning we could not envision continuing this arrangement indefinitely. It became unthinkable to contemplate planning future operations along these lines. After all, there were children from the drive-in church families who were attempting to learn their Sunday School lessons around splintery picnic tables, with thumbtacks holding down their coloring papers from strong winds. Unexpected showers would send the little children scrambling, dripping and shivering into the shelter of the family car! So we dramatized the problems.

We dramatized the real honest, human problems: a woman without any legs who could only worship in the drive-in church seated in a little basket! A paraplegic with his wheel chair folded in the back seat. ''These people have a right to a church of their own,'' we suggested. So you must similarly dramatize your problem until it is honestly emotionalized!

3

Help your people to take the long view of the problem.

Enable them to see down the long road ahead through projected studies of the future. Show them that the problem will not disappear by ignoring it. Ask the question: will the problem go away if we do nothing about it?

For instance, we pointed out to our people in Garden Grove that the drive-in theater where we worshiped had refused us a lease for our Sunday use of their facility. We met there on a week-to-week basis only. Any Sunday we might be told that we could no longer conduct church services there. Should that happen, and our growing congregation suddenly be evicted, we would become spiritual refugees on the edge of the freeway. What an embarrassment to Jesus Christ's program this would be!

4

Now ask everyone to join in giving God a chance to work a miracle if this is what He wants.

Taking the long look, it was easy to point out that the drive-in theater might not want to keep us on indefinitely as permanent residents. And, as it turned out, this supposition proved correct, for ten years later, swap-meets became a highly lucrative business at this very drive-in, as well as at other outdoor theaters. It was only a matter of time before we would have been moved out anyway.

Cost account the solution to the problem. Ask the question: Will the solution come cheaper if we wait 5–10 years? In most cases this will get action NOW! If the ready cash is not available NOW ask for freedom to find a solution to the money problem.

It is most unlikely that a majority of people would resist a motion to ''give God a chance to work a miracle.'' You may have to communicate to your people an awareness of

101

how the money problem can be met. Here you simply exercise possibility thinking yourself.

Calculate how money can grow. You can begin a fund with $5. Calculate how easy it is to build a fund of $5 into $100. What are all the possible ways in which you could raise money to build a fund to $100 and what are all the possible ways to increase this $100 to $1000? What if you added $1000 a year for five years? What if you made it $5000 a year for ten years? What if you made it $10,000 a year for twenty years? What if you made it $15,000 a year for thirty years? What does it add up to?

You may have to show them how, if you increase your parking lot by 100 cars, you can increase your church families by 100 families a year, each contributing an average of $450.00 a year, which adds up to a gross annual added income of $45,000.00. Multiply this by twenty years and what do you come up with? Actually, you should formulate and mimeograph these figures and distribute them to your key men.

5

Now offer various creative solutions to the dramatic, emotional, factual problem.

In our case, we called a congregational meeting and I explained that the routine of conducting two church services in two separate locations was unthinkable. I would not, and could not, contemplate being the pastor of two separate, growing churches. I had been called to organize *one* church.

I offered three solutions:

Solution One: Drop the drive-in ministry work and let the sick and the handicapped, the old and the infirm, go home and listen on the radio the way they do all across America.

Solution Two: Separate the two institutions into two separate organizations, each with their own pastor. I would resign from both situations so both groups could start fresh without my personal leadership.

Solution Three: I offered to merge both churches into a single new creative development to be known as a "walk-in, drive-in" church.

I then proceeded to show all of the advantages of the third alternative. I pointed out how this could become a truly large church with a great program for people of all ages. If the churches separated, I told them that it was my opinion that the little church in Garden Grove would never be able to expand beyond its two acres and would always be a mediocre, medium-sized church in an ever-growing town. "It would be like shooting elephants with a .22 single-shot rifle," I warned.

I emphasized that if we merged, we could build something great, something powerful, something pacesetting, something exciting and something that could be helpful to thousands of people. At this juncture, I opened the floor for questions.

Not surprisingly, one of the first questions raised was: "Reverend Schuller, where do you expect to get the money to buy the land, not to mention all of the buildings, that you're talking about?"

To which I replied—as you must reply—"Our job is to be great thinkers for and with God. We must trust God to provide if He wants to have this. Our God is not a pauper.

"My Bible says that 'my God shall supply all your need according to his riches' (Phil. 4:19). The Bible also says, 'If you have faith as a grain of mustard seed, you will say to this mountain, "Move...," and it will move; and nothing will be impossible to you' (Matt. 17:20, *RSV*).

"The question is not: *'What will it cost?' The all important question is: 'Would it be a great thing for God?'* If so, I am sure that He will find a solution to the financial situation if we give Him time."

There were a few other questions raised. At this point, Dr. Wilfred Landrus, one of my leading laymen, rose and quietly read from a small slip of paper a resolution that he had been scrawling with a ball-point pen. It read: "I move, Mr. President, that this congregation go on record under God as favoring the merging of the two churches in a new development."

Immediately that positive motion became the leadership of the moment, proving again that the man who makes the positive motion is the leader! It was immediately seconded. Then there was time for discussion.

Parliamentary procedure was rigidly adhered to under my chairmanship. No one was permitted to speak more than twice for or against the proposal.

The motion was put to the house. It was passed by a vote of 54 to 48. The decision was made. The idea was virtually sold!

Make sure the top positive thinkers in your congregation are alerted in advance and are behind you all the way.

Tap the most trusted, competent, positive, enthusiastic lay leaders and privately advise them of what "God is leading you to lead with." Prayerfully draw them into a circle of confidence and trust. Ask them for their support.

Tell them you need them. You do! Tell them God needs them! He does!

Be honest—don't be a manipulator. Tell them why you have called them into this inner circle. "I trust you. You are a big person. You are able to envision possibilities; you are able to imagine solutions to problems; you are able to move forward with a daring faith.

"You are the kind of men that are needed to fill the lay leadership vacuum in this church. God is counting on you. I am counting on you!"

Now present your recommendation to the official board —or to the

When you are assured of their support—and guided by their wisdom, then lay the idea before the board and one of the positive laymen will make a motion, while a second supports it. And the idea is about to become a decision!

Reread now the steps of how to sell your ideas successfully. Always begin with *Step 1:* make sure your idea
solves a real problem. Talk about the problem. Always
follow this with *Step 2:* dramatize the problem as exten-
sively and emotionally as possible. Follow this immediately with *Step 3:* taking the long view.

*congregation —and
make the decision
a definite
commitment.*

Now move on to *Step 4:* showing your solution, and
asking people to join in giving God a chance to work His
miracle. You are then ready, presumably with key laymen
deeply involved in advance, for your strong leadership
thrust.

In my personal experience, I have always found it very
helpful and advantageous to give the initial promotional
thrust to the entire congregation in the form of a sermon.
My congregation expects me to be their leader. They are
not offended if I launch a sermon and (a) show the problems that are facing our congregation today, and (b) show
how these problems are going to get worse, and (c) show
how there are several solutions, but here is the best one of
all!

I advise them that this is what we're going to give God a
chance to do! I tell them we're going to move ahead in
faith and expect miracles to happen! This makes for very
positive, inspiring and highly motivating sermons.

You'll have to judge the tempo of your own situation and
determine if this is the way you wish to handle it, or if you
prefer to have your official decision-making board approve it first, and then present it to the full congregation in
the form of a sermon. With the purchase of the
$1,000,000 ten-acre piece of property adjoining our orig-
inal property, I took it first to the church board. Then, with
their approval, I presented it in the form of a sermon to the
congregation. It was the right way to handle it at that time.

The next steps are very simple. All you have to do is to
start a fund if your idea is going to cost money. And then

105

hire an architect if your idea calls for the construction of a building.

"But how do you handle the impossibility thinkers? What do you do with the obstacle people who insist on obstructing your plan, your project, your dream?" This is a question I am often asked by ministers who attend our institutes. In answer, I say, "Make sure, first of all, that Christ is the head of your church and in the master role over your personal and private life. It is my belief that sometimes God allows our dreams to be frustrated because we are not ready for success if it happens immediately."

Here is my testimony:

I had successfully "sold" the concept of a walk-in, drive-in church to the congregation. They voted by a slight majority to adopt the policy of working toward a merged church. Up to that point, I had succeeded.

However, the opposition was deep-seated. Its members refused to concede defeat. They were instrumental in bringing in the first staff addition to our church—a man who was not my personal choice. The opposition gravitated toward him and used him as their negative leader.

Nothing is more difficult than trying to maintain the momentum of success-producing enthusiasm when there is a serious split within a church. Well, I had this experience! Those were the dark, despairing months of my life.

When I could tolerate it no longer, I prayed a very deep prayer, "God, I can stand no more of this. I don't know who is for me and who is against me. I am asking You for Your help. If You want this church that we envision to be built, then You will have to solve this problem. I can't."

The next thought that flowed into my mind was the Bible verse—and I heard it clearly emphasized: "*I will* build *my* church!" (Matt. 16:18).

I leaped to my feet, and perhaps over-dramatically,

threw a gesture to my empty office chair and said, "Then, Jesus Christ, do it! You be the head of this church. You take command. You solve the problems. And You handle the problem people. And if You don't mind, Lord, I'm going on vacation. I'm tired."

When I returned four weeks later, I discovered that the staff minister had been called to another field of work and had accepted the assignment. The opposition had lost its leadership. But the parting pastor challenged the congregation to "beware of a man who only preaches positive thinking and doesn't preach the full gospel of Jesus Christ." So the obstacle people continued to hang in there until they saw themselves truly defeated.

The truth is that God used that difficult experience to wrestle ultimate leadership from me! I think I really thought I was *the* leader. From that moment on, the center chair at my board meeting has been empty. Christ is the *real* Chairman of the Board.

How do you handle negative thinking obstructionists? Begin by surrendering your innermost self—and your church to the Lordship and leadership of Christ. Now follow these tips on handling impossibility thinking laymen.

1

Don't attract them to the church.

You attract negative thinkers by preaching negative sermons. I think of one minister of a particular church that has been analyzed by our institute. This minister's sermons are consistently negative. For about two years, he was anti-Catholic. Then, for several years, he shifted to anti-Communism. Next he became anti-ecumenical. Finally he became anti-glossalia.

During every one of these phases, he attracted into his congregation people who were inflamed against certain issues. That's like putting carcasses in your backyard and then wondering why you attract vultures instead of hummingbirds. You need to hang out hummingbird feeders to attract hummingbirds!

2

But if you have impossibility thinkers in your church, don't feed them.

Then they will wander off in their hunger. If you are not already aware of it, you will soon discover that most impossibility thinkers are neurotic negativists. A neurotic negativist needs to be fed a negative sermon constantly. Stop preaching negative sermons, and negative thinkers will become "hungry for the whole gospel" — what they really mean is "hungry for *bad news*" — and they'll wander off to some pulpit-pounder down the street!

3

Don't build a stage for these negative people.

If you have them in your church — and every church does have them — don't create an opportunity for them to sound off. *Robert's Rules of Order and Parliamentary Procedure* is so designed that the president of the corporation and the chairman of the board can keep impossibility thinkers from disrupting the meeting or taking the reins.

You simply do not appoint an impossibility thinker as the chairman of a committee. It's amazing how many ministers do this, thinking that they will "win the man's favor and convert him." That's like suggesting that your daughter marry a crook in order to convert him!

You build a stage for impossibility thinkers every time you give everyone in the congregation the chance to express their opinions on a controversial issue. You build a platform for the impossibility thinker to sound off, to gain support for his negative position, when you publicly ask for everybody's opinion on an upcoming decision! Furthermore, this is not "democracy." This is indecisive, uncertain, insecure leadership.

4

Know when and how to confront those obstacle people.

When and *how* should they be confronted? And *who*

should do the confronting? To find the answers to these questions, go to the one, two or three most loyal, most Christlike positive thinkers in your congregation and seek their advice.

Generally speaking—and it would be a rare exception when this principle would not hold—the pastor should never confront the negative-thinking, obstructionist layman. Another layman should do the confronting and spare the pastor. Not for the selfish reason that a pastor is unwilling to suffer the scars of battle, but for the sake of the church.

There are times when a confrontation must take place. This should be done by the strongest and most prominent, positive-thinking layman in the church. When it is done and how it should be handled is something that must be prayerfully thought through in every individual case. Perhaps the impossibility thinker may have to be frankly advised to "resign from the church board." If the decision has been made to move ahead on a major project or projects, he has no right to continue to be an obstructionist!

In many instances, the obstacle person can be replaced by a full-time or a part-time staff member who is hired to fill the slot that the impossibility thinker occupies. And, of course, your bylaws will specify that the senior pastor approve all additions to the staff and will have a hand in selecting them personally. In this way, a positive thinker can be placed in the position.

Work now to attract possibility thinkers.

Ultimately, the congregation will be overpowered by possibility-thinking church members. A young minister at one of our institute sessions returned to his eastern church with great enthusiasm. However, two weeks later, he was rudely treated by one of his key laymen.

He complained about it to his wife and her reply was,

"Dear, you made him into that kind of a person by the kind of sermons you've been preaching ever since you've been here. You've been preaching negative sermons, critical sermons and 'here's-what's-wrong' kind of sermons. He is only giving back to you what you have been giving to him."

Now, this pastor is involved in developing in-depth, possibility-thinking treatments throughout the church. It's a lengthy procedure, but given enough years possibility thinkers will be attracted and they will win out.

Entrench
possibility
thinkers in
power positions

Bylaws can help you here. Remember that in your bylaws the minister is an ex-officio member of each committee. The minister also appoints the chairmen of the committees. The bylaws require that no new business will be handled or heard in the board meeting except if it comes as a positive recommendation from a standing or special committee. That means that committee meetings are the place to nip impossibility thoughts in the bud, before they reach the church board.

Your bylaws will also specify that you have the freedom to build a staff, subject to the board's approval. You select both the staff and the key men on executive committees. The staff then becomes a committee of its own with the power to offer recommendations to the church board.

If some impossibility thinker speaks up at a board meeting with some negative idea, you as board chairman can handle his suggestion very skillfully and sweetly by "referring the matter" to whatever is the appropriate committee. Or you may decide to refer it to the staff for their study with instructions to report back at a later date. If you fail to specify a time for the report to be returned, the negative proposal can simply die in committee.

Meanwhile, you will make sure that your committees are staffed by powerful possibility thinkers.

Positive ideas outlive negative ideas. Positive ideas thrive on enthusiasm. And enthusiastic people have more energy, live longer and generate more force than negative-thinking personalities.

Great positive ideas never die. People may quit on the idea but the idea seldom, if ever, quits by itself. So have faith, my friend!

8
*Do keep showing
nothing but love
for the
impossibility
thinkers.*

If you allow hate thoughts, resentment thoughts or other negative thoughts or emotions to dominate you, these emotions will show up in your words or in your life. And you will lose ground as a result! "Whom the gods would destroy, they would first make angry" is an old Greek proverb.

Keep cool. Remain Christlike. And the majority who have backed you so far will continue to love you. Your love for the impossibility thinkers may not convert them, but it will keep them from winning added support.

Whatever you do, continue to practice the power of possibility thinking! Keep believing in the promise of Christ who said, "If you have faith as a grain of mustard seed, you will say to this mountain, 'Move...,' and it will move; and nothing will be impossible to you" (Matt. 17:20, *RSV*).

Now, forget about the obstructionists. Go on adding and winning new members to your church. Your new converts will soon outnumber, outvote and overpower the opposition.

Chapter 11

How You Can Make an Inspiring Impression

It was 1955, and I had failed to find an empty hall to rent anywhere in all of Orange County. So I finally turned to a drive-in theater for a place to begin holding Sunday services. Then hearing of this turn of events, the ministers of the First Methodist Church, the First Baptist Church and other established denominational churches of Garden Grove extended their sincere sympathies to me.

Yes, my wonderful friends in the ministerial association genuinely felt sorry for me. Why? In that drive-in theater, I would have no roof over my head, no pews for people to sit in and no classrooms for Sunday School purposes. Moreover, we would be located outside the eastern city limits of Garden Grove.

What have you got going for you?

The other churches all had the advantages of buildings, pews, organ and Sunday School classrooms. And, for the most part, they were located in downtown Garden Grove. Yet even as they were sympathizing with me, I replied, "But don't feel sorry for me. After all, I have three things

112

going for me in the drive-in theater that none of you have.''

"And what are they?" the pastor of the Methodist Church asked.

"Number one," I answered, "I have superb accessibility. The Orange Drive-In Theater is right on the Santa Ana Freeway, and that's the heaviest traveled road in the State of California. People can drive twenty miles in twenty minutes and be at my church. Nobody has a better road leading up to their front door than I do! And you have to have a road leading up to your front door before you need a building.''

"Number two, I have virtually unlimited parking space. I could invite the biggest crowd-getter in the world to speak in the Orange Drive-In Theater and not have to worry about turning people away. We have parking for

1700 cars!'' I pointed out that the existing churches in Garden Grove had virtually no parking lots whatever. Furthermore, the seating capacities of their churches were decidedly limited and they wouldn't be able to consider inviting ''great crowd-getters'' if they wanted to.

"Number three, I have a much larger market than you men do. You are in the heart of one town. I am on a main road which intersects three large cities—Anaheim, Garden Grove and Santa Ana!

"You are at the heart of a town; I am at the heart of a county. So, don't feel sorry for me. I have a vast market of unchurched people to reach. All I have to do now is make a big, beautiful, successful and inspiring impression on all of these non-churched people in the county and we'll build a great church for our Lord.

How do you make an impression?
Some months after we had launched our church services in this drive-in theater, I wrote a letter to Dr. Norman Vincent Peale, the most sought-after speaker in America at that time. I wrote to him as follows:

"Dear Dr. Peale,
I would like to invite you to be a guest speaker in our church some Sunday. It is the largest church in Orange County, with parking for 1700 cars! It is a most unusual church. Everyone who comes has a soft upholstered seat by an open window, with a view of the blue sky and orange trees that encircle the property. On a spring morning, the fragrance of orange blossoms saturates the area and literally creates a heavenly aroma. And while we worship, the soft sunlight streams into our assembly. We are located on the busiest road in the State of California. Assuming that every parking space is filled, we are talking about a potential audience of nearly 6000 people!''

114

Inviting Dr. Peale was my attempt to impress un-churched people in my community. I knew that the un-churched people in Orange County were not impressed by my name. I was a nobody. They would never cross the street to come to hear me. But they were reading Norman Vincent Peale.

Somehow I had to make a big, walloping impression on the whole county to let everyone know that (a) I was in business; (b) this was an inspiring business; (c) we were a successful business; (d) we were really going to town and they ought to get on the bandwagon. By inviting Dr. Peale, I hoped to convey these inspiring impressions to unchurched people in Orange County, California.

I was delighted when Dr. Peale accepted my invitation! I was not dishonest. He knew full well that we were conducting services in a drive-in theater.

The morning of his appearance arrived. *The Power of Positive Thinking* was Dr. Peale's most successful book and it appeared on the best-seller list at the time he visited our church. As a result, there was bumper-to-bumper traffic up and down the freeway as cars flocked into the Orange Drive-In Theater. When eleven o'clock arrived, the place was jammed with 1700 cars, plus cars parked in the aisles! What an enormous array of vehicles!

Dr. Peale and I sat on steel folding chairs atop the snack bar of the drive-in theater. My wife played the two-manual electronic organ that we pulled on a trailer every Sunday from our home three miles west of the drive-in theater. The organ music was pumped directly into the sound system and then through private speakers into the indi-vidual cars. A choir, imported for the occasion since I had no choir of my own, sang through microphones and pro-vided the choral music. Another microphone in front of the pulpit carried my voice through the theater's sound system into each car.

Introducing Dr. Peale to the great congregation, I began, "I am so delighted to announce that we have with us this morning the man who, in my mind, is the greatest positive thinker alive in the world today. Everyone knows his name. Most of you have read his inspiring words. I hope that many of you can make his personal acquaintance this morning. If you get to meet him personally, you will never be the same. He brings the greatness out of you! His name . . . is Jesus Christ.

"And here to tell us all about Him is Norman Vincent Peale!"

It was at this very moment in modern American church history that Dr. Peale was beginning to be the subject of attack by both the conservative and liberal elements of Protestantism. I was warned not to invite Dr. Peale to the church because "the fundamentalists of the area will think that you are not really fundamental." And the friend went on to say, "And the liberals will all make you out as being too conservative."

To all this, I replied, "I am not interested in impressing Christians of the conservative or liberal persuasion. I am here only to impress non-churched people. And Dr. Peale is widely read by non-church persons.

"Furthermore, I am interested in building a church that can put 'strong wings on weary hearts.' I am also interested in attracting positive-thinking, enthusiastic people into the membership. I believe Dr. Peale is precisely the right man to invite! He will make the kind of impression I want to make on the non-churched community."

My observation proved most accurate. For twelve months after that service, we took in hundreds of members into the church who came originally to hear Dr. Peale speak "in person."

"Who are you trying to impress, Schuller?"

Many years later after we had our own church built, I

116

was walking across our magnificent grounds and ran into a wonderful old farmer from the Middle West who had stopped by to "see what this big deal was all about." With enthusiasm, I ushered him around the area. I took him into the pulpit of the sanctuary, pressed a button, and we watched the glass walls slide open. "This makes it possible for people in the drive-in church to see me at the same time people in the sanctuary have visual communication with me," I explained.

Then I flipped a switch and twelve fountains leaped into being out of a block-long pool of water. I took him through the gardens and up and down the Tower. When I finally wound up this personally conducted tour, my visitor looked me full in the face and asked me the cutting question: "Just who are you trying to impress, Schuller?"

Up to that moment, no one had ever been that blunt with me. It was brutal, but it was the greatest thing that could have happened! It forced me to analyze our motives.

I gave him an honest answer. "We're trying to impress non-Christians and non-churched people. We are trying to make a big, beautiful impression upon the affluent non-religious American who is riding by on this busy freeway.

"It's obvious that we are not trying to impress the Christians! They would tend to be most critical of the expenditure of money we have made. They would tell us that we should give this money to missions.

"Nor are we trying to impress the social workers in the County Welfare Department. They would tell us that we ought to be content to remain in the Orange Drive-In Theater and give the money to feed the poor. But suppose we *had* given this money to feed the poor? What would we have today? We would still have hungry, poor people and God would not have this tremendous base of operations which He is using to inspire people to become more successful, more affluent, more generous, more genuinely unselfish in their giving of themselves."

As a result of our experience with the old farmer, we formulated in the Self-Study Guides distributed to participants of our Institute for Successful Church Leadership this revolutionary question: "Who are *you* trying to impress?" After having studied many hundreds of these Self-Study Guides, we can report on the answers to this all-important question.

It is obvious that the average pastor in the average church is not making an all-out effort to impress the non-churched people — or his church would have more unchurched people in its pews and in its program.

Some ministers are subconsciously trying to impress the minister who originally impressed them as young boys. "I have always held in my mind the image of my dear old pastor," one minister said to me, "and I wanted as a young boy to become a preacher who would preach the kind of a sermon that would draw praise from the pastor I admired." He continued, "As I analyze my sermons, I find that I am really subconsciously trying to impress that dear old pastor who, incidentally, died many years ago!"

Other ministers are trying to impress their theological professors. Subconsciously, they are still striving to get a top mark in their class on sermonizing! So their profound vocabulary of theological and biblical terms is designed to impress — not the unchurched persons — but the enlightened theologian.

Still other ministers and church leaders are trying to impress the "bishop" or the "top executive officers of the denomination." They very carefully take public positions and decide how to vote on controversial issues, based upon what kind of impression this would make on the leaders of their denomination. They are consciously or subconsciously thinking that they may be promoted to a bigger and better church if they make a good impression on their superiors.

The weakness of this kind of thinking should be transparently clear. In the first place, a man ceases to be effective when he dishonestly seeks only to impress his peers. This is not the way to build a church! Your denominational peers are not going to get converted, move out to your community, join your church and make it grow.

If you, pastor, can impress the non-churched people in your community, your church can grow faster until you will have, by the blessing of God, a better church than the denomination could ever turn over to you! And, meanwhile, you will have been honest to your own convictions and will not have become a politically ensnared tool of an ecclesiastical machine. Be your own man, under God!

Still other ministers are seeking to impress the Christians who move into their communities. Again, this becomes obvious by simply looking at the sermon titles in the average church page of the community newspaper. You'll find, for the most part, that they are designed to impress religious people.

When we started our church in Garden Grove, God gave me the common sense to understand that I should never expect to win the Presbyterians, Methodists, Episcopalians, Lutherans, Baptists, Seventh-Day Adventists, Congregationalists, the Open Bible people or members of the many other groups. After all, if they were already members of one of these denominations, they could be expected to join the local denominational church of their choice. Why should they switch? Why should they join our church? And if they did, what gain would that count for the kingdom of Christ?

Our only hope of building up a vital and growing church is to impress and win non-churched people. To that end, everything was designed from the very beginning to make a big impression upon the kind of non-churched people who lived in our area. This is the only way any minister can make a church grow.

And the good news that I have for you is that your church—unless it is located in a tiny town in a rural section—is unquestionably surrounded by a vast majority of people who are not committed to any faith, to any religion, to any denomination! *That means that there is an enormous potential for your church growth.*

There is a great market for your product! All of these people—although they may not realize it—really want the gospel of Jesus Christ. So go to work and attract these people. Be an inspiring impression-maker!

How do you impress unchurched people?

Sincerity impresses!

Begin by trying to impress them with your sincere desire to help in solving their personal daily problems.

Ring doorbells. Some minister asked me how to spell the word success and I replied, "W-O-R-K!" I rang more than 3500 doorbells the first twelve months I was in Garden Grove.

I made an all-out effort to impress people with my willingness to help them with their daily problems. I made an all-out effort to impress them with my sincere desire to be a helpful and friendly human being in their community. Obviously, this pays off! But be sincere. People can spot a phony a mile off.

Success impresses!

Then seek to make an impression of success.

The first service of worship we conducted in the drive-in theater was a service where we used *printed* morning programs. From the beginning, I have refused to use mimeographed Sunday bulletins. A mimeographed bulletin says, "We can't afford to print our Sunday bulletins and we save a lot of money by mimeographing them."

I was insistent upon creating a success image in the very beginning and, therefore, I allocated, from the slim resources at my disposal, twenty dollars to have the morning church bulletins printed by a very fine printer. I still continue that policy. The quality of your church bulletins, the photographs used, the caliber of the music you select, the architecture of your buildings—all of these things create an impression, be it good or bad.

When we were to build our beautiful walk-in, drive-in church a half-mile west of this drive-in theater alongside the same heavily traveled freeway, I determined to hire the finest architect I could possibly find. I was well aware of the fact that, in attempting to create something entirely new—a walk-in, drive-in church—the project would have to be executed in such excellent architectural taste that we would not be shot down by critics, but would be praised for the quality of the design.

Beauty impresses!

We selected Richard Neutra, who took my original drawings of the walk-in, drive-in sanctuary, the fountains, the pools and the tower and sketched them out in an award-winning concept. It was another attempt on our part to make a favorable impression on non-churched people. And it worked! Architectural magazines in several languages around the world published stories about the church, and pictures of it appeared internationally. As a result, non-churched people interested principally in architecture came to our property just to see the building, and many remained to hear our message, accept Christ and become vital members.

Multiplied millions who drive by our church are attracted to the sight of a huge cross on top of a 15-floor tower. The top of the cross reaches to a height of 252 feet above the ground. It is the tallest cross (90 feet) to stand on any cathedral tower anywhere in the world.

I have been deeply influenced by Richard Neutra. We worked closely together for twelve years planning and building our walk-in, drive-in church. Together, we agreed upon the principles that were to be carried out in our church architecture. "The secular and sacred must be integrated in architecture," we both agreed. Therefore, we deliberately designed clear glass windows so people seated in the pews can see "the world out there."

A religious experience that is experienced in the sanctuary does not seem totally divorced from daily life if, out of the corner of your eye, you can see a jetliner gliding through the sky at the moment that you experience Christ coming into your life. In the distance, you can see cars moving over a bridge on the busy highway at the very moment the pastor is praying. The evolution of your soul and spiritual life is more significant and beautiful when integrated with the secular world.

Meanwhile, non-churched people who come to the church are impressed. One can enter into many sanctuaries where all sorts of profound symbolism is woven into the architecture. This may have real meaning to the Christians. But if the sanctuary is designed first of all to impress non-churched people, then it must be remembered that these meaningless symbols only confuse and distract the non-Christian.

There are those who argue this point with me. But I know of no one who disagrees with my position on this issue whose church is growing faster than ours! And I have observed that those who quarrel with this position on church architecture and insist on letting it be dark and gloomy, resplendent with all sorts of mysterious symbolism, are themselves pastors of churches that are not for the most part meeting with enormous success in winning and converting the unchurched person.

Again the question must be raised: "Who are you trying to impress?"

Mr. Neutra made an interesting point to me one day. "Why," he asked, "did churches ever get into the custom of building structures that obstruct from their view the outside, secular world?"

I offered the usual answer. "I suppose it comes from the concept of God being in the sanctuary or in and around the altar."

He enlightened me. "But Christians sought fellowship with Jesus on the mountaintop, in the out-of-doors. They had experiences with Christ under the open sky and in the sanctuary and on the beach. Then why did Christians develop the kind of church that they did?"

He proceeded to answer his own question. "In the early days, the Christians were forced underground. They worshiped for generations in the catacombs. Here, in dark underground caverns, candles were required to give light. Consequently, little children, with their impressionable childish minds, were raised to have religious experiences in a setting where the world was shut out and only candles flickered. The altar was frequently a coffin or a platform designed for a coffin. These were the natural niches in the hallways of the below-ground catacombs.

"So, when these Christian children became adults and finally emerged into the sunlight with freedom to build churches above the ground, they designed the structures that would recreate what, in their minds and experiences, was a religious mood. It had to be reminiscent of the catacomb setting. Consequently, the buildings were designed to be dark, with flickering candles on a gloomy altar at the end of the corridor."

Even today, the typical building committee of a new church attempts to design a sanctuary that fits their religious childhood impression of what a church should appear to be. So, in planning a church, *they are unconsciously seeking to impress those who were raised in a church — instead of trying to design a structure that would make an impression on non-churched, secular Americans.* One of the great tragedies is right here. Hundreds of thousands of churches are designed to stimulate, not the positive emotions of joy and hope that come with the fall of sunlight in the room; rather they are designed to stimulate the negative emotions of darkness, dreariness and gloom! I have sadly advised one church to sell its new structure because the emotional statement of the structure is so negative it is impossible to feel joyful in that building!

When Mr. Neutra suggested that he would like to set the stone *vertically* on our building, I immediately agreed. He explained, "Stone is always set horizontally or random, but the new international style, with its aluminum, steel and sheets of glass, has created magnificent vertical lines. It seems to me that we should continue the theme of verticality by setting stone in a vertical manner. After all," commented Mr. Neutra, "you don't wear a club-stripe tie with a pin-stripe suit."

And so our church became the first building ever designed anywhere in the world where stone was set vertically. As a result, this made a big impression on architects, builders, contractors and the masons themselves. Photographs appeared all over the place! People came to see the beautiful buildings, with their vertical stone; and some of them returned on Sunday mornings and joined the church!

Modernity impresses!

At this point, many churches suffer from terrible errors of design judgment. I ride past many old churches with their dated architecture. And I feel painfully sorry for the pastor who is trying to impress modern, unchurched people — when the biggest impression he is making in the community is colored and influenced by an out-of-style, out-of-this-world architecture.

Such a church announces to one and all: "This church is old-fashioned, out of date, from bygone generations without any exciting plans for the future." Is that what your church architecture says? If so, you have a problem.

And this brings up a principle from which our Institute for Successful Church Leadership never wavers: the growth of the church is the only thing that matters. Money does not count. Winning people to Christ is all that matters. If a church structure stands in the way of growth, then remove, remodel or relocate the structure!

Honesty impresses!

In designing a church building, a church program, a church advertisement or a church organization, you must be an inspiring impression-maker. And you must impress people with your honesty. There have been many mistakes in church architecture. For example, not a few un-churched people who come into a church are impressed—negatively—with the phony props that adorn the auditorium; the artificial lighting; the carefully contrived staging; the sentimental-solemn effect. These features are obviously designed to manipulate a person's emotions into an unreal religious mood.

Non-churched people see the phoniness of this. One of these people said to me after having been in such a sanctuary: "I felt like I was in a religious night club. I go to one night club that has an African motif. I go to another bar that has an Old English motif. I am thinking of another restaurant I sometimes patronize. It has a Hawaiian mood. Now, in all of these places I am emotionally conditioned to believe, for a fleeting moment, that I am in Africa, England or Hawaii.

"Then, when I went to that church with its dark walls and deeply stained windows and indirect lighting on an illuminated cross with flickering candles, I felt as though I were in still another world. It's contrived. I felt manipulated. It's a phony setup."

The same man who made that remark came to our

church and was impressed by the honesty of the entire architectural arrangement.

Superb architecture seeks not to impress people with ornamental beauty. Rather, the structure hopefully becomes inconspicuous and nature becomes the center of attention. And so, one is impressed with the sky, the water, the flowers, the trees and the green grass. All of which means that the structure becomes a vehicle for effective communication.

Richard Neutra taught the doctrine of bio-realism. According to this doctrine, man was designed by God with a built-in tranquilizing system. Eyes look upon rounded hills, sweeping green pastures and tranquil pools of water, and man's nervous system responds by producing a feeling of deep relaxation. The church building, it follows, should be a vehicle for effective communication between God and man, and between man and his fellowman.

Effective communication is a process whereby a positive suggestion is placed in a suggestible mind and is received therein. God designed the human organism in such a way that when we are deeply relaxed and very calm, we become receptive to an outward suggestion. (And that is nothing more than a form of hypnosis!) Medical doctors do not use the term "hypnosis." They describe this state as "deep relaxation."

So the doctrine of bio-realism would say that a church building should be the kind of a structure where man, upon entering, feels tranquil, calm and relaxed. He will therefore be in a mental mood where he will be receptive to outward suggestion, respond accordingly and make commitments. With this objective, the structure should not seek to excite, but to tranquilize. That is why Mr. Neutra deliberately avoided bright colors, which tend to excite, and held to more natural, organic colors which tend to tranquilize.

Who are you trying to impress? *Your church will grow*

126

if you are trying to impress non-churched people. Be an inspiring impression-maker and watch your church go to town!

*Impress
the community*

How can you impress the non-churched people in *your* community? That's for you to find out. If you make enough calls on homes, you will begin to catch a reading.

Find out where the unchurched people in your neighborhood are hurting. Where do they experience difficulties? What are their daily problems? What are their needs?

Find the honest answers to these questions, then you will know how to impress them. You will then be able to design the program to meet their needs and their wants. And when you put this kind of a program into operation, you will be swamped with success!

Discover the mood of your neighborhood. Who are the heroes of your community? Who are the civic leaders, the writers, the actors and other prominent personages that the unchurched people in your community admire? Grab hold of the coattails of these heroes. Invite them to your church. Use them unashamedly! Your job is to impress the non-churched people in your community.

I discovered one day that there were over 1300 medical doctors living in Orange County, California. About that same time, I ran across a newspaper article which proclaimed, "Newly elected president of the American Medical Association is an unusual man. He happens to be a successful physician and at the same time is a very ardent churchman, teaching Sunday School every Sunday." I immediately wrote a letter to the doctor and invited him to be a guest lecturer in our pulpit.

When he accepted, I sent a letter to all the members of the American Medical Association in Orange County, inviting them to hear the newly elected president of the medical association. They were impressed. Many of the doctors who had never come to our church to hear Dr. Schuller speak, or even to hear Dr. Norman Vincent Peale speak, did come to hear the new president of the AMA.

On another occasion, I discovered that there were over 3000 life insurance salesmen in our area. "Who is the man that life insurance salesmen would come to listen to?" I asked myself. I came up with the answer, "W. Clement Stone." I managed to get an acceptance from Mr. Stone.

Then we mailed a letter to all of the life insurance salesmen, as well as a letter to all of the securities sales- men in the area. And they were impressed! Many of them came simply to hear a man whom they had heard about and admired.

Impress
the unchurched

The secret of winning unchurched people into the church is really quite simple. Find out *what* would im- press the non-churched people in your community and find out *who* would impress them. Find out what kind of *needs* exist in the private lives of the unchurched people in your community.

Discover the *cultural tempo* of the unchurched people. Then forget what Christians may think. Forget what your denominational leaders might think. Go out and make a big, inspiring impression on these non-churched people! And they'll come in! And when they do, may they find the beautiful Jesus Christ living in your life and in the lives of the people in your church. When they find the beautiful love and joy of Christ, they will never want to let it go.

Success, for God's glory, is in your hands right now, if you follow through on this question: *"Who are you trying to impress?"*

128

Chapter 12

Three Keys to Certain Success

Inspiring preaching! Exciting, human-need-filling programs! Enthusiastic advertisements and publicity! These are the three miracle-working keys that can unlock the doorway into a fantastic future for your church!

I instruct ministers who attend our Institute for Successful Church Leadership to "send me copies of the three most outstanding sermons you've ever preached." And if there is any one statement that covers most of these sermons, it is simply that they are *sermons preached* by *preachers*. Yet, if we are truly interested in impressing non-churched people, we must realize that the secular society has a deep-seated negative impression of "preachers" and "sermons."

So, many more years ago than I can remember, I stopped referring to myself as a "preacher" and my morn-

Inspiring preaching

129

ing messages as "sermons." Our morning bulletin simply states, "Morning Message." As a layman in our church once explained, "Schuller doesn't preach. He witnesses."

You see, the average non-churched person envisions the preacher as someone who offers only a red-faced verbal spanking from the pulpit, his sermon little more than a scolding, finger-pointing, wrist-slapping, pulpit-pounding rebuke. And quite probably, a study of the sermons preached in the sixties throughout the United States of America would justify this image of Protestant "preaching." In those days, unchurched people, perhaps facing a personal or family crisis, would enter a church on Sunday only to hear a judgmental, suspicion-producing sermon on, "Why a Christian Must Advocate the Admission of Red China to the United Nations." And had they entered the church across the street, they would probably have had another sermon preached with equally negative intensity on, "Why a Christian Cannot Remain Silent on the Admission of Red China to the United Nations."

In an earlier chapter we outlined our case for never using the pulpit for controversial issues. The truth is that no man is preaching the gospel when he stops giving people exciting and inspiring good news from the Sunday pulpit! People will rush to hear exciting good news!

Unless you have some good news every Sunday morning, pastor, you are not prepared to speak from the pulpit. I don't consider myself prepared to enter the pulpit on Sunday morning unless I can share some exciting experience I had with God over the past seven days, or a work I saw God perform in a human life in a daily life situation!

That's keeping the gospel up-to-date. That's keeping good news as alive as today's newspaper. And this is what the world desperately needs!

When we began our church in the Orange Drive-In Theater, I had accessibility, surplus parking and good news every Sunday! And my messages have continually stressed the upswing of life. While many Protestant pastors suffer from a neurotic anxiety over the tormenting question of "how can we be relevant to today's world," I recall the words of Richard Baxter in his Yale lectures saying to students a few hundred years ago: "Boys, preach to broken hearts and you will always be up-to-date!"

I have enormous confidence in the power of the spoken word when it conveys good news—its power to sway, to influence, to mold, to change lives! Recently, a non-churched family in southern California lost their four-year-old child in their backyard swimming pool. Carrying their grief, they went to a church hoping to find comfort and consolation, but they only got a social-political harangue. Then they found a church that was able to put "strong wings on their weary hearts." They stayed, they were saved, and they are serving today!

In the *Christian Herald* of October, 1969, the late Louis Cassells talked about the "Protestant Blahs." In a perceptive article, he analyzed the problems facing the modern church. He wrote: "A professional man of Bethesda, Maryland, told me he had quit going to church because 'it seemed kinda pointless to sit there Sunday after Sunday while the preacher bawls me out for attitudes I don't have'."

Another letter, in the same article, is from a woman in Columbus, Ohio, who writes, "We are tired of being told from the pulpit that we have been coming to church all our lives for the wrong reasons—such as because we wanted to belong to a country club, or to build a fancy building, or to take shelter away from the world's troubles."

Then Cassells came to the theme of the article: "That brings me to what I consider to be the most important reason why people are drifting away from the Protestant

131

fold. *They haven't found in church what they hoped to find—a confident faith in God.''*

And in the same article, the author quotes the Methodist theologian, Dr. Albert C. Outler: ''The middle class is reacting to the way we have assumed they were the golden goose and the whipping boys at the same time. They are fed up with the general disposition of the church to scold them rather than minister to them.''

Finally the author concludes: ''Many middle class churchgoing families don't necessarily disagree with——they may even heartily approve—the stand their pastor takes on Vietnam or race relations. What distresses them is the feeling that the pastor is so preoccupied with the plight of distant people who happen to be black and poor that he completely ignores the urgent personal problems of his own parishioners who happen to be white and a little better off economically. Genuine agony of mind and body and spirit can exist in a suburban rambler as well as in a cold-water flat.''

And finally: ''Let me emphasize that I (Louis Cassells speaking) am not contending for one moment that ministers should be less concerned with the needs of the poor and oppressed. I am simply arguing that they *also* should display a little compassion and pastoral concern for human suffering which they can discover, if they will only take the trouble to look for it, in their own flocks.''

At the beginning of the decade of the seventies, *Look* magazine had an interesting symposium contributed by a variety of thinkers in our country. It was an attempt to analyze the problems of our world at the beginning of a new decade. Near the close of the issue, they got to the root of it all when they said, ''Joy is the missing ingredient in our culture—the healing force that can join individual impulse with a common good.''[1]

In the same article, Vincent Harding wrote: ''In most of America, there is no sense of joy at all—that is, apart

132

from age four down. A society that I am seeking is a society where joyousness is a part of the very fabric of life. I want a society in which people can touch each other without fear."

Oddly enough, the one institution, namely the Christian church, that traditionally specializes in generating joy, building faith and spreading optimism, is the institution that seemingly has been affected and afflicted in the second half of the Twentieth Century with cynicism, bitterness and negativism. So the world goes hungry for the joy and the faith that the good news of Christ can offer.

Somehow, we must discover the enormous power there is in the real gospel of Christ. When a minister steps into a pulpit with genuine enthusiasm, exciting energy, positive statements of hope, people will flock to listen.

I recall attending the World Psychiatric Congress in 1967 in Madrid, Spain. At the closing session, there was a round-table discussion on the subject: "Human Values in Psychotherapy." The first lecturer, Dr. Rome, past president of the A.P.A., spoke for thirty minutes on the subject, "Faith." In effect, he said that it was the duty of the 4000 psychiatrists from around the world to build faith in the hearts and lives of their clients, since the traditional faith-building institutions no longer seemed to be carrying out this vital function!

He was followed by a second doctor from Germany who spoke for thirty-five minutes on "Hope." He discussed the enormous healing power of hope: "Many of us have had patients who sat under our analysis for months without any sign of recovery until, one day, a spark appeared in their flat, dull eyes: it was the spark of the birth of hope! And healing began in that miracle moment!"

The third lecturer was from Lima, Peru. Believe it or not, he spoke on the subject, "Love." He said: "Nothing is more powerful in its healing potential than non-judgmental love. Non-selective, non-judgmental love is the greatest healing force in the world."

I went out of that assembly depressed — and in the next moment, overjoyed! Overjoyed that I had discovered the reason why our church was growing by leaps and bounds! We were meeting human need on the deepest level because our morning messages were consistently designed to build faith, generate hope and illustrate vital, non-critical love. But I was also depressed because I could see the Protestant church declining in America for the simple reason that most ministers did not understand this very simple secret of successful preaching!

I had learned this lesson myself the morning that I introduced Dr. Peale to that great drive-in audience. After the elaborate introduction that I gave him, Dr. Peale stepped to the podium and looked across the more than 1700 automobiles jammed with people and said: "What would Jesus Christ have to say to you if He could stand here and talk to you through me?"

He boomed out that tremendous question, waited until his voice had moved out into the surrounding orange groves, and then he continued, "Would He tell you what miserable sinners you are?"

He paused again and then continued, "No, I don't think so. I don't think He would have to tell you what sinners you are. I think you would know it. I think He would immediately begin telling you what great people you can become if you will only let His Holy Spirit of faith, hope and love fill every ounce and fibre of your being!"

Well, that sermon by Dr. Peale changed my style from "preaching" to "witnessing." Until that moment, I looked upon the job of a sermon to be fundamentally directed to generate a sense of guilt in guilty hearts! What I failed to realize was that unchurched people, who have no vital relationship with God, have a much deeper sense of guilt than we Christians realize. It is this sense of guilt that keeps them out of the church, the same way an overweight man avoids stepping on a bathroom scale!

Dr. Peale had said to us in his unforgettable sermon that Jesus Christ never called a human being a sinner. That really shocked me! I went home that day and read the Gospels from Matthew through John, because I was convinced that Dr. Peale had made a mistake. And, in truth, I discovered that all of the "sinners" that He met—like Matthew and Peter, Mary Magdalene and Zacchaeus— were not condemned as sinners, but were actually or indirectly complimented by Christ! Only the holier-than-thou hypocrites received the stinging rebuke from Him.

Now—here's how you can preach to pack your church with unchurched people:

1. Don't "preach sermons."

You can introduce people to the distinctive beliefs of your church after they enter your pastor's classes, but *don't try to sell them on your peculiar doctrines in a sermon on Sunday morning!* They are not ready for it yet.

Let your Sunday morning services aim at inspiration, entertainment and a basic commitment to Jesus Christ. Then get them into a small classroom setting where they will be more receptive to the deeper doctrines of your church.

Witness to the experience you had with your God this past week. If you've had no experience with Him, the chances are you were not calling on the sick or counseling with the troubled!

2. Don't be controversial in the pulpit.

Save that for a small group meeting where there can be respectful dialogue which alone leads to conversion of attitudes. In controversy you may relieve your frustration,

and you will certainly earn enough opposition to boast that
you are "being persecuted for righteousness sake." But
you will—in almost every instance—do your "cause"
more harm than good!

3. *Always be positive.*

Make every sermon you preach positive. How can you
tell if it's positive? Simply by asking yourself, "Is this
stimulating positive emotions?"

Remember, too, that humor is a positive emotion. It is
healthy. It is healing. It is unifying. It is harmony-
creating.

There is a great deal of therapeutic and spiritual value in
wholesome entertainment that comes in the form of warm
and wonderful humor. So work at it. Make your sermons
fun to listen to. Make them a positive witness!

Your hardest job will be resisting the constant tempta-
tion to "attack the enemies you see in the world." Remember, until you are able to verbalize your concern in
the form of a positive, inspiring idea or dream, until then
you are ill prepared to speak out!

4. *Let every message stimulate the positive emotions of the listeners.*

Positive emotions are: love, joy, peace, kindness, gen-
tleness, goodness, faith, hope, humor, aspiration, trust,
respect, self-confidence, enthusiasm, ambition, courage,
optimism! Never play the negative emotions—fear, sus-
picion, anger, prejudice, sorrow, despair, self-hate, pessimism, etc.

Make your list now. See how many positive emotions
you can identify. Now make an equally long list of negative emotions and vow never to let your message—or
your pulpit announcements, or the words of the anthems,

hymns, or prayers—be allowed if they send out and stimulate negative vibrations.

Follow this advice. Keep it up week after week, year after year, and you will literally transform the personality of your congregation! It will be fun to go to your church!

5. *Keep your messages well illustrated.*

Remember we deal with people who are too busy to think—they have time only to pick up on impressions. We deal with a graphic mentality, not a logic mentality. Communication that is effective draws a big picture, then adds a short sentence.

Billboard advertising is the best illustration of how to communicate from the platform that addresses people who are living and thinking at a fast pace. The most effective messages will have three or more sharply identified points that can be made in a sentence or two, then illustrated with honest down-to-earth, positive, emotion-generating stories. Then they are summarized with a powerful one-liner for emphasis.

6. *Be sure to aim every message at some specific human problem.*

Remember the theme of this book, the secret of successful churchmanship: find a hurt and heal it.

7. *Don't be afraid of repeating yourself.*

It's impossible for a minister to "preach the same sermon" over again! You'll be a different person the second time around. Your listeners will have changed too! So I have a message—every year—on "How to Overcome Fear" and another one on "How to Find Peace of

Mind.'' The message takes a totally new meaning in each new phase of life!

8. *Never "preach" on something you don't feel very strong about!*

And people will marvel at your week-after-week enthusiasm and sincerity—two of the most important ingredients of successful speaking. So the place to start looking for sermon ideas is in your heart—not your head! Use your heart first, and your head will follow!

9. *Good sermons are like great architecture: "Make it strong but don't let it feel heavy." A second architectural principle also applies: "Form must always follow function. Never reverse the order!"*

In other words sermons are designed to help someone function! I've heard miserable messages that were form first—beautiful poetry and snobbish quotations full of ego boosting and name dropping. They served more to self-congratulate the speaker than to serve the hurts of the listener.

10. *Expect positive results.*

A minister once fell into depression because, he confessed, ''I've preached for years and nothing seems to happen.''

''Tell me,'' his sympathetic listening friend asked, ''when you go into your pulpit and while you share your thoughts do you *expect* anything to happen?'' That question pointed up the pastor's problem!

If your message begins with your heart—aims at a real human problem—and *concludes with a call to decision*, then you can and will expect positive results. It is this positive expectation that will make your message sound like it comes from an excited young person standing on tiptoes! Plan your conclusion carefully and design it to call your listeners to a personal commitment and the dynamism of great expectations will inject real vitality throughout the whole service!

11. Always lead people to Jesus Christ!

It's really true—unchurched people are fascinated by this famous name. A missionary to Japan said to me, "It's strange—people here don't want to hear about Christianity although they are really interested in Jesus Christ."

"Then don't preach Christianity," I advised. "After all, Christianity is like all religions full of shortcomings, sins, and hypocrisy. But *do* preach Christ! Tell the world about Him!

"Live so close to Him that He is your dearest Friend. Invite Him to live in the front and back corners of every drawer in every room within your mind. And when you speak it will be Christ speaking, smiling, loving, and laughing and uplifting the hearts of listeners.

"There is, after all, one unfilled need that exists in every human heart every Sunday. Every Christian and every non-Christian comes to church needing a fresh encounter with the inspiring, encouraging, new-hope-producing Spirit of the Eternal God. Bring Christ alive into their minds and hearts and you'll be a winner in the pulpit!"

12. Build people—never destroy them!

One of the most moving spiritual experiences of my life stemmed from the musical production, *Man of La Mancha*. For suddenly I saw the man of La Mancha as an allegory of the Christ. He is such a positive thinker! When he sees a prostitute, he lauds her as "My Lady."

She, wild-eyed, almost bare-breasted, open-mouthed, leers at him, saying in a voice filled with mocking disbelief: "Me a lady? I was born in a ditch by a mother who left me there, naked and cold and too hungry to cry. I never blamed her. I am sure she left hoping that I would have the good sense to die."

The man of La Mancha continues to look at her, continues to believe the best of her, continues to appeal to her subconscious, self-image as he announces grandly: "Your name is not Aldonza. I give you a new name. You are my lady. And I give you the name 'Dulcinea'."

She later appears in hysterics on the stage, having been raped in the barn by rough travelers. The man of La Mancha again affirms his belief in her goodness.

But, wounded, crushed, filled with self-hate, she screams at him: "Don't call me a lady! God, won't you look at me! I am only a kitchen slut reeking with sweat! A strumpet men use and forget! I am only Aldonza. I am nothing at all!" And she runs off the stage.

As she makes her exit, he calls to her, "My lady!" And after a short pause, looking out into the shadows, he again calls, "My lady!" And off in the stillness, he calls out the new name he has given her: "Dulcinea!"

At the conclusion of the play, the man of La Mancha is dying of a broken heart. At this point, a strikingly beautiful Spanish lady approaches his bedside. "Who are you?" he asks with the feeble voice of a dying man. She has been kneeling at his side.

Now she arises, stands tall, and with queenly beauty announces: "My name? My name? My name is . . . Dulcinea!"

The work of redemption is complete! A self-hating, self-loathing, self-condemning person finally comes to believe that she can be beautiful and wholesome and lovely! You'll fill your church with unchurched people if you'll build them into the faith that through Christ they too can be beautiful.

Inspiring preaching must be backed up by exciting programs designed to impress non-churched people of every age. And the Number One program of any church is the church school or Sunday School.

If you are sincerely interested in winning non-churched people, you should seriously consider scheduling your church school at the same time church is going on. We have discovered that non-churched people are interested in having their children go to Sunday School even if they don't attend church services themselves. Early in our ministry, we found that some parents would drive their cars into the church property, drop their children off and arrive later to pick their children up again.

So we scheduled adult church services at the same time that Sunday School was going on and discovered that almost all of these non-churched parents stayed for worship! It was more convenient than going home and coming back! And because our worship proved to be exciting, inspirational and entertaining, they not only stayed——they also enjoyed it. We found that our church school program did succeed in bringing the non-churched person into the pew on Sunday mornings.

Next we scheduled two morning services and two sessions of Sunday School, thereby getting twice the mileage out of all our physical facilities. Today we conduct three sessions of church school *and* three morning church services, all operating concurrently at 8:15, 9:30 and 11:15 A.M. By offering the full Sunday School program at each of those times, we obtain triple utilization of all our educational facilities! At the same time, we schedule our children's choir rehearsals at 10:00 A.M. So a variety of combinations can thus be offered to people, meeting almost every conceivable requirement of many different life-styles of people in the community.

Programming the church school obviously requires strong leadership on the supervisorial level. The Protestant church has yet to learn the importance of hiring staff people in the role of supervisor. We can envision hiring a minister of education, but in the typical church he is the only person hired to handle all of the administrative details of the church school, including the recruiting and training of teachers, supervision of the library, the allocation of class space, and so forth. As a result, he simply will not have the time to give the close supervision over the teachers that this kind of activity demands.

We have made the discovery at Garden Grove Community Church that to hire a chief executive to head a department—without hiring the adequate supervisorial help on the managerial level—will prove to be inadequate and unsuccessful. Precisely for this reason, many staff situations fall apart. And the blame is too often placed mistakenly upon the minister of education, or the senior pastor, or the "failure of the people to respond and support him."

We can learn a great deal here from business, industry and the military organization. In the military, there may be a single general, but he needs colonels to inspire the majors with his orders, majors to inspire the captains, captains to inspire the lieutenants, lieutenants to inspire the sergeants, sergeants to inspire the corporals and the corporals to inspire their small squads of privates. Notice that between the general and the squad there are several levels of full-time, professionally-staffed supervisorial officers.

We may look upon the head of a department as the idea-generating power-plant! The several levels of employed staff persons (unless you are fortunate enough to have extremely talented and dedicated volunteers) are

142

booster stations to "pick up" the power-generated idea from the head of the department and transmit it along down the line without allowing any of the power to be lost along the way. Very, very few church schools in America have been adequately staffed in this manner.

No wonder the Sunday Schools are falling apart! The army would fall apart, too, if it were as inadequately staffed as the church school. And the army has the power of unchallenged authority, with disciplinary powers to back up its authority!

Somehow, Protestant church planners must discover this principle: *ideas lose their enthusiasm-power unless recharged by personnel operating on a supervisorial or managerial level.* Consequently, in our highly effective church school, we have an enormous staff. They are outstanding people.

Under the direction of such a competent staff, church school and youth activity programs are planned for children and adults of all ages. We have classes for almost every type of person. We have a class for mentally retarded children. This fills a vital human need. After all, they can't be left in the regular nursery.

We also discovered very quickly that our community has a number of single adults. Consequently, we organized a "singles" group. It has been said that Garden Grove Community Church was the first church to have a full time minister to singles. It wasn't until we had passed the 5000 membership figure that we had enough single adults in the various age brackets to closely grade this program—which is vital to real success. We now have a group of singles in their twenties, singles in their thirties, another group in their forties, and still another group of single adults in their fifties and up. The key to a successful program is to sharpen it, focus it, and grade it as closely as possible!

Program your church for institutional success. I marvel

at Dr. Harold Fickett, pastor of the successful First Baptist Church in Van Nuys, California. I have often had him lecture at our Institute for Successful Church Leadership simply to explain the unbelievable variety of clubs and organizations in operation at his church. I believe he even has a bowling league for the deaf. He applies a basic principle of successful retailing: he is increasing his inventory to meet a greater market!

Remember what we have already said elsewhere in this book: make a careful study of your larger city, county or community and you can begin to identify the kind of programs that will meet and fill human needs.

Enthusiastic publicity

If you have inspiring preaching and exciting programming, then all you need is enthusiastic publicity and your church will break all growth records!

The first thing I did when I came to Garden Grove to launch a new church was to spend fifteen dollars for a small mimeograph machine large enough to take a postcard. Next I spent another forty dollars for a hand-operated addressograph machine. Then I began ringing doorbells, picking up names and addresses of any unchurched persons in the neighborhood that I could lay my hands on. I began building the mailing list!

Yes, before I held even my first service in Garden Grove, I picked up all the names and addresses I could. And all were added to the mailing list. Remember: *a mailing list is all-important. It is your first line of publicity. It is the way to build a church!*

Our most prized possession in the Garden Grove Community Church today is not the $250,000 organ or the $1,000,000 Tower of Hope. Rather, it is the 7000 families who make up our mailing list!

The second thing I did was to prepare an advertisement for the newspaper: "Come as you are in the family car," the ad read. "Starting Sunday, March 27, 1955, an exciting new church will begin to operate in the Orange Drive-In Theater!" The Sunday morning bulletins were printed, as were the registration cards, to give the impression of a successful, going organization.

Immediately after our first Sunday in the drive-in theater, I sent out a postcard to everybody on the mailing list with an enthusiastic, success-predicting announcement: "Nearly half a hundred cars drove quietly into the beautiful setting of the Orange Drive-In Theater this past Sunday to launch what may well become one of the great churches in the world." And with that immodest, enthusiasm-generating announcement, the people on the mailing list were led to believe that this was going to be a winning thing and that they had better get on the bandwagon right away!

Through the years, the strategy has always been as follows:

1. The newspaper advertisement published every Saturday is geared to bring non-churched people into the church. The ads are generally built around helpful sounding messages.

2. People are urged to register their attendance. The object is to get them on the mailing list!

3. The mailing list is worked weekly to build church attendance the following Sunday. This simple procedure, followed year after year after year, is the one single, simple secret of effective publicity at Garden Grove Community Church.

Not always do we place the ads on the church page. When Dr. Peale was to speak in our church, we advertised on the woman's page, knowing he had a following there; on the business page, including the West Coast edition of the *Wall Street Journal,* and on the sports page. We assumed that if we wanted to impress non-churched people we would have to put the ads elsewhere than exclusively on the church page.

For the first six years of our church in Garden Grove, I made it a point—religiously—to go to the office on Monday morning and begin the week in the following manner:

First, I would write the copy for the weekly card that was to go out to the entire mailing list—a message geared to generate enthusiasm for the coming Sunday. Next, I would dictate or draft a news release which was later mailed to area newspapers—an article describing events planned for the upcoming Sunday. I would then lay out the ads advertising the messages to be presented during Sunday's services.

Personally, I feel that it is enormously important for the senior minister to be in charge of the publicity program of the church. By being personally responsible for the publicity, I was forced to create, produce and generate sermons and programs that were newsworthy and had real publicity value! And when I really felt that we had to break into the headlines, it simply meant that I would have to make every effort to bring some famous personality to our "unlimited parking" church, be it Norman Vincent Peale or Catherine Marshall!

A very important question in the Self-Study Guide prepared by those who attend our Institute for Successful Church Leadership is: "How much of your church income is budgeted for advertising?" The answers are astounding! We recommend a minimum of 5 percent of the church budget for publicity purposes. If the church is ailing or struggling, then it had better go considerably higher.

Our first service of worship in the Drive-In Theater was held on March 27, 1955. By December of that year, we had taken in a little over $8000. But during that same period of time I had reinvested in newspaper and radio

146

advertisements over $4000! That's 50 percent of the income put back into publicity!

Let the following principles guide you as you plan enthusiasm-generating publicity that will pack your church!

Expect a very small return.

That means you must think in terms of reaching thousands of people with advertisements if you want to win 10 to 100. Most churches fail in publicity because they do too little and go into it too small.

Remember that good advertisements never cost —they always pay.

All you need to do is win one family and their tithe or their offering over a period of three or four years will more than pay for the entire cost. The last item to be cut from the budget should be this money-producing item. That's what advertising is!

Consider a radius of ten miles from your church as the drawing power of your congregation.

Many ministers fail because they think that people won't drive more than two or three miles. Nothing is further from the truth in today's world.

Aim at saturating the area in the 10-mile radius.

Don't worry about competition with other churches. If people are interested in another church they won't come to yours anyway. Meanwhile, your advertisement will help create a general momentum in the community which will say: "Religion is really alive out here!" And the other

147

churches will indirectly benefit more than they realize! Your advertisement will only challenge other church members to be more active in their own congregations.

Advertise when people are in a buying mood.

In other words, you don't try to sell air-conditioners in December, but in the heat of summer! So plan your heaviest advertising in the seasons of the year when the non-churched people might conceivably be interested in attending church. This means, of course, a saturation campaign the week before Easter. For years we have sent a brochure to every home within a 10-mile radius of the church heralding our Easter services.

I discovered that in our community, as in every community of America, there is a business called "direct mailing." This type of business has the addresses of all the residences in the city and county.

We discovered, in working with the firm, that there were 130,000 homes within a 10-mile radius of our church, so we budgeted $5000 to send an Easter invitation to each of these homes.

We became so excited, knowing that we were inviting 130,000 families, that we scheduled three services on Easter instead of two! We estimated that perhaps $1000 would come in the form of extra offerings and we figured that if we won only ten families from the 130,000 invitations, those ten families would give an average of $5000 a year, paying for the entire project in twelve months' time! Of course, it worked out much better than that! A friend of mine, Rev. Guy Davidson, founder and pastor of a fantastic, successful church in Tempe, Arizona, advertises very heavily in the summer months because, "That's when most of the homes change hands—new people are moving in between the end of one school year and the beginning of another."

148

Determine the mental attitude of your area and analyze what would impress the unchurched people in your community.

Then let your advertisements portray the kind of an image that could appeal to these *unchurched* people. I am often asked for samples of our advertisements. I always refuse. They were geared to impress a certain *type* of person at a specific *time* in history. Each pastor must research his community *today*.

In setting up any publicity material, do not try to impress Christians or religious people.

They are already involved with the church. Concentrate on the 50 percent who are non-committed to any faith.

Select sermon titles that will appeal to the unchurched. Consider a series of sermons and advertise them over a six-week period. In the first ad, you can announce the six titles. Try to appeal to the unchurched people on the level of their thinking and self-interests.

A suggested sermon title might be: "How to Make Marriage Succeed in Today's World." The title sounds like an article from a secular magazine. It actually sounds quite nonreligious, but you can put plenty of the Bible and Christ into it.

The idea is to get them to come to church in the first place! And if they are not interested in religion, chances are that they won't be attracted to church by religious-sounding titles.

Make certain that all of your publicity creates an image of your church that says:

- This is a positive-thinking church.

- This is a church that really believes in the power of Christ to transform human life.
- This is a church that welcomes everyone no matter what his background.
- This is a church that believes in building people up—not tearing people down.

Continue the job of advertisement and publicity until you are reasonably sure that every household in a 10-mile radius knows and understands that:

- You are in business.
- You are offering distinctive services that nobody else is offering.
- You have something they need.

So publicity is never finished. There are always people moving in and out of the community. Furthermore, as the church moves along five years, then to ten years, then to fifteen years, new and bigger programs of community service, education, evangelism and counseling will be offered which will require wholesale communication.

Follow the above public relations and advertising principles and, provided you also have inspiring sermons and exciting human-need-filling programs, this enthusiasm-generating publicity is guaranteed to make your church boom!

Footnotes

1. *Look* Magazine, January 7, 1970.

Chapter 13

Fund Raising
Can Be Fun

It is the contention of the Institute for Successful Church Leadership that *no church has a money problem; they only have idea problems!* Big, inspiring, human-need-filling ideas are money-makers! Successful goals always produce their own financial support if they're widely and enthusiastically publicized! Only fear, small faith or timid thinking can cause failure.

So fund-raising really becomes fun!

Now, don't ever use the lack of money as an excuse for not beginning! Remember—*it doesn't cost a dime to dream!* It doesn't cost a dime to stand in your inspiring pulpit on a Sunday morning and preach a sermon to your people on the subject: "How to Make Your Dreams Come True," and then honestly lay before them the inspiring dream that God has given to you for the church where you serve!

151

Now that you have a dream, and assuming that your great goal has passed the success-spotting principles, move ahead with great faith. In all of your money-raising activities, follow these principles:

Remember that you will never get money from people by scolding, generating guilt feelings, or perpetrating other negative insults.

I once heard a minister offer this horrible prayer when the offering was dedicated to the Lord in a church service: "Here, Lord, in spite of all we say and do, is what we really think of You." It was a dirty dig, a cheap insult. Clever? Yes! Sharp? Indeed! But also stupid! There are many people who were not able to give what they wanted to that morning. You never generate maximum response by a negative approach.

Remember that you can spoil the whole "money tree" if you give the impression that you are having financial problems!

Nobody likes to invest in a shaky business. Plead and beg and you will only reveal your weakness. And a weak institution does not inspire generous contributions.

There were times in the history of our church when we were really fighting for enough money to pay the next week's bills. Then, before the Sunday offering, instead of laying this weakness before the people and throwing *my problem* upon the tired shoulders of the persons who came to church to *unload* their problems, I made a statement to this effect: "You people are wonderful. You come here week after week and give so generously, even though we never appeal and plead for your financial help. You are simply thoughtful and generous folk.

"There have been times when we were desperate for

financial help. We prayed to God. We trusted Him and always He was able to meet our needs through wonderful people like you! I just felt this morning like I wanted to tell you how grateful I am, and how I love you for what you are doing! May God bless you! Thank you again. Now, let us worship God with our tithes and morning offerings.'' That approach has always been successful.

Remember that you will spoil the money tree if you go after small pickings, such as suppers, sales and second offerings.

At the outset, Mrs. Schuller and I, as the only two members of the church, established the policy that we would never attempt to raise money through bazaars and similar affairs. We would rather, once a year, frankly, openly and honestly, lay before our people a beautiful surprise package filled with exciting ideas that they would want to buy! And we'd give them a chance to buy it! They would make their pledges of financial support and we would carry out our church year from this response. And a simple little financial appeal a week or a month or two months before the annual financial appeal would be enough, we knew, to stunt the whole tree!

To achieve maximum response, you must let everyone know that you are counting on them —and on them alone!

Make it clear that you are not going to receive financial support from the denomination in the form of federal charity; you are not going to ask local businessmen to support your project; and you are not going to make appeals from the pulpit on Sunday morning! To do so would only create an image that you are not financially strong, and it would, at the same time, frighten off the non-churched person who is coming to church to seek strength and not to be weakened by listening to someone complain about his financial difficulties.

Again, remind yourself that the only way to generate maximum financial response is to throw out an exciting, inspiring human-need-filling, problem-solving project.

Give your people a tremendous dream and an enormous and inspiring challenge—and they will love to give! Help them to *visualize* and *emotionalize* the project!

Never be afraid to ask people to give money for a great cause.

It is important to have a sense of timing here. Obviously, timing will vary from situation to situation.

In our experience at Garden Grove Community Church, we have been reticent about asking for financial support more than once a year. There have been rare exceptions when we interrupted the year for a special financial campaign. When an important opportunity came along, we did not allow it to keep us from giving God a chance to work another miracle through the people.

However, as a matter of policy, *we generally restrict ourselves to a once-a-year appeal. Then we give it all we've got!* We open up with all the power at our disposal.

The point here is: don't be afraid to ask people to give money for a great cause. People love to spend their money. They can't wait to spend it on a new car, a new house, new clothes, anything that excites, stimulates or inspires their imagination—or offers help and healing and hope to their family, marriage or private life!

A great project for the church is exactly what people want. They can't wait to give generously toward it! One illustration here might be helpful to you. The roughest job

I ever had was trying to raise $1800 for a dishwasher in the kitchen of our church. It was far easier to raise a million dollars for the Tower of Hope! Or a million dollars for a new ten acres of property! Big, imaginative, problem-solving projects really turn people on!

Every year you must offer some new challenge in the form of a new program, a new project, a new building, a new addition to the staff or a new missionary project.

Every year you *must* add something *new!* If you fail to do this, you are saying to the people: "We have stopped. We are moving backward. We can't move ahead. We have run out of great ideas!"

You are making this growth-retarding decision based on *your negative assumption* that God has no other possible sources of financial aid to meet your increased budget! If you cannot add something new, you are not growing. If you are not growing, you are not living on the edge of exciting faith! And you are not giving God a chance to perform His miracles!

Now, you must get organized to communicate this exciting challenge to the people in the most effective way.

In our church, we have always had an annual "every member" canvass. On four special occasions in the first 15-year history of the church, we employed professional fund-raisers to organize and communicate financial challenge to the people. Without exception, these proved to be exciting experiences. Some people did object. But we refused to surrender leadership to the hands of objection-minded people! Rather, they—for the most part—were caught up with new life, new enthusiasm, new excitement as the projects moved along.

In later years, the techniques of "organizing to communicate effectively and inspiringly'' shifted from annual ''every member'' visitations to an annual church dinner. We did this in the fall, generally in November. The congregation was invited to be the guest of the church for dinner. We selected the finest restaurants in the finest hotels in the entire area. Beautiful decorations, inspiring entertainment, made it an exciting fun night. There was music, there was laughter, there was great inspiration. It became a tradition as ''the great night out for everyone.''

At this dinner, the people were given an inspiring, challenging look at what surprises the budget for the new year held for Jesus Christ. In portraying our message, we used graphic slides projected in multi-media on a huge screen. The entire program of the church, from janitor to missionary, was emotionalized and dramatized through color graphics.

The congregation was then informed that the budget could be raised—no matter how impossible the task looked.

The program then called for a quiet moment of dedication as everyone was invited to sign a pledge card, fill in the amount, drop it in the offering plate as it passed.

And so, in one fun-filled, inspiration-packed, forward-looking, mountain-moving night, the church took another giant step upward! *This was done every year!*

Our 15th year—1970—marked our first departure from the traditional dinner. We simply did not have room for the anticipated crowd. However, we carried out the same program, in effect, renting the Convention Center in nearby Anaheim, and we had 6800 in attendance. A producer and director were secured to write a fast-moving, one-hour music-and-humor-filled show. The show led up to my slot where, for twenty minutes, I unfolded with word pictures the tremendous challenge of the new year, with its greatly enlarged budget, and led the attendees to the signing of their pledges.

156

The point is, something that entails such a concentrated effort must be done annually!

Always, on the Sunday before your pledging party, emphasize tithing. Emphasize it throughout the season.

By that, I do not mean two or three "messages on money." On the Sunday before the annual dinner, I preach my "once-a-year message" on tithing. I warn the people before I begin by saying: "Isn't it wonderful to come to this church week after week, Sunday after Sunday, and never hear a word about money? There is only one Sunday a year when I talk about it. Of course it takes money to run a church. But we don't raise it through special appeals, extra offerings, pitiful or scolding announcements every week!

"Once a year, I share an exciting promise that God has given to us in His holy Scriptures! It's the most fantastic key to financial security I know of! Let me tell you about it." And I launch into my annual tithing talk. At the same time of year, members of the congregation are also receiving tracts on tithing through the mail.

Weekly offering envelopes are mailed to all of those who pledge. A follow-up letter is mailed to all who do not pledge at the annual "night out," and not a word is ever mentioned about financial needs again until the next year!

And so, for fifty-two weeks people can attend the church without being badgered for tickets to this supper or donations to that cause!

Our financial success seems to prove the assumptions of the Institute for Successful Church Leadership that people will give all you need if you focus on real solutions to real needs and present the story in a positive, inspiring and enthusiastic way! Remember, Jesus said: "Ask and you shall receive; seek and you shall find; knock and it shall be opened unto you'' (Luke 11:9).

Never let money problems stop you. They may delay you but don't let them defeat you. Remember—nobody has a money ''problem.'' It's always a *symptom,* not a problem. The real problem is lack of dynamic, need-filling ideas, a lack of courage and nerve or a lack of faith!

Don't ever again use the lack of money as an excuse—unless your God is terribly poor. Mine isn't! We found that out as we raised several million additional dollars the first twenty years for capital financing. When we needed to raise money for land and buildings, for more land and more buildings I found out the biggest problem every time was not God's power but my feeble faith!

And as you read ''The Garden Grove Story,'' you'll see what I mean.

Chapter 14

The Garden Grove Story

When the little church I had served for five years in Chicago heard that I was leaving to begin a new church in California, they gave my wife and me a farewell gift. It was a check for approximately $300, enough to make the down payment on a two-manual electronic organ.

Getting started

During the first year in my Chicago pastorate, I went home on a number of occasions to my relatives in Iowa and literally begged them for gifts of money toward the purchase of an electronic organ. Now that I was going out to start another church from scratch, I was determined to do two things: begin with an organ and begin without mimeographed Sunday morning bulletins!

So enroute from Chicago to California by car, we stopped at a music store in Iowa run by an old friend of mine, Howard Duven. He agreed to take the check from the Chicago church as the down payment on a two-manual organ, with the balance to be paid off in thirty-six monthly installments of thirty-eight dollars a month. With a salary of $4000, I calculated that my tithe would make the monthly payments.

Enroute to California, I practiced possibility thinking and made a list of nine possible places in which to conduct services: (1) rent a school building; (2) rent an Elks Hall; (3) rent a mortuary chapel; (4) rent a Masonic Hall; (5) rent an empty warehouse; (6) rent a Seventh-Day Adventist Church; (7) rent a synagogue; (8) rent a drive-in theater; and (9) rent an acre of ground and pitch a tent.

We arrived in California and were given a check for $500 by our sponsors, the denomination. I brought the check to a local bank and opened an account there under the name of "Garden Grove Community Church." (I didn't think the name "Reformed" would bring the *unchurched* people rushing in!) Then I began working my way through the list of possible sites for holding church services.

Within a week after arriving in California, I had already exhausted eight of the possibilities I had considered for holding services. I finally came down to the one that read "rent a drive-in theater." So six days after our arrival, I went to the Orange Drive-In Theater and asked the manager if I could use his place for Sunday morning church services.

He obliged, and I asked him what it would cost. "Oh," he said, "let's say $10 a Sunday which is what I have to pay the sound man to come out here to throw the sound control switch on and off."

I now began to spend the $500 that was in the church checking account. For $25, I had a four-by-eight-foot sign

160

painted, posted on a triangle and set under a palm tree in front of the drive-in theater. The sign announced that services would be held in this place every Sunday morning at 11 A.M., starting Sunday, March 27, 1955.

Next I spent $75 for a microphone which I could jack into an outlet of the sound system on the sticky tar paper roof of the snack bar of the theater. The plan was that I would stand up there, speak into the microphone and address the people who would be listening through the private speakers placed inside their automobiles.

I proceeded to spend another $110 for rough lumber which was delivered to our small house. There in our one-car garage, we stored our mahogany organ while awaiting the grand opening! And here, with only a hammer and saw, I began to build our first altar and a 15-foot cross.

Hard work

My next item of expense was $25 for a used trailer upon which I placed the organ, pulling it behind my car every Sunday from the garage to the drive-in theater. I didn't realize then that I would do this for more than five years!

Then I proceeded to spend about $50 for brochures. Hoping to impress non-churched people, I wrote to Dr. Norman Vincent Peale, who wrote back a marvelous statement with his permission to quote extensively. So I grabbed hold of his coattails, and we proceeded to buy advertisements in the papers.

By the time the first Sunday arrived, we'd spent almost the entire $500! But it was the beginning of something great! To our delight, we received $86.78 in that first offering.

From the very beginning, I was able to promise the people that they were ''most fortunate to be a part of an

Exciting programming

161

exciting program that God was moving and planning in Orange County!'' I believed it. I felt it. I knew it. And this conviction spread through the lives of those who listened.

Now, with the financial support of the denomination, two acres of land were purchased at a cost of $4000. And the church extension committee announced that one of the local ranchers ''who puts up buildings on the side'' had agreed to ''design plans for your church for nothing.'' I gasped! I was a student of architecture, and to me this was intolerable!

I asked the extension committee to loan me the money to hire an architect. They refused. ''We've never spent money for an architect yet and we're not about to begin now,'' was the verdict. To which the spokesman for the group added: ''We just can't afford to hire fancy architects.''

Bold planning   On my own initiative, I proceeded to contact a young architect in Long Beach. ''My name is Robert Schuller,'' I wrote. ''You don't know me, but I'm an honest man. I'm 28 years old, and I'm starting a new church. Its building must be designed by a good architect.

''I know what we want to build. Will you draw the plans for me? I promise you that you will be paid in full. I'm not sure how much I can pay or when you will get paid, but I guarantee that you will be paid completely in my lifetime.''

Richard Shelley took a chance. He drew magnificent plans and submitted his first bill. It amounted to $1000. I announced to what was already a growing congregation in the drive-in church that we would need to raise $1000 for the first payment to the architect who was designing our new church. We took a special offering and the $1000 was given!

When the last of the total fee of $4000 was due, he

submitted another bill. I challenged the people and they responded. He was paid in full and on time!

Obviously, there was a great deal of prayer involved in all of this. And obviously we moved ahead with possibility thinking, believing that it would be possible to accomplish our objectives. We proceeded to build our first $70,000 unit on the two-acre parcel of ground. We were about to increase our corporate debt from $1600 (still owed on the organ) to nearly $70,000. But this was not done until I received pledges from the congregation assuring us of an increased weekly cash flow to cover at least the *interest* on the increased debt!

Much prayer

163

It was about this time that I was called to a nearby rancher's home and Warren Gray introduced me to his wife, Rosie. ''She's been sitting in your drive-in church every Sunday since the beginning,'' he told me. ''She can't walk and she can't talk. She can only grunt and drop a tear. You see,'' her husband explained with moist eyes, ''my wife Rosie had a stroke a few years ago. And the drive-in church was just the answer for our needs.''

When I left the Gray ranch, it was with the understanding that they were to join the church the following Sunday and would be baptized. This was exactly at the time when the pews were being installed in our pretty little chapel in the lovely suburb of Garden Grove. The question naturally arose: ''Now that we have Rosie Gray, a handicapped old lady as a member, what are we going to do about the drive-in church when we finish and open our new chapel in a month?''

The board quickly made the decision with my enthusiastic approval: it was decided that I would conduct a service at 9:30 A.M. in a new chapel and then go to the drive-in theater to hold an eleven o'clock service for Rosie Gray. Soon she would die, they reasoned, and we could discontinue the work. Deep in my heart, though, I wondered if I would ever be able to give up what the drive-in theatre offered: fantastic accessibility—and a parking lot big enough to invite Norman Vincent Peale to appear in!

As it turned out, Rosie Gray kept living—year after year, and both churches grew in both places. And the dream unfolded in our imaginations of a sanctuary where people could sit in a traditional pew arrangement, while others would sit in their cars parked in a landscaped drive-in church. It was an intriguing plan.

Finally, by a narrow and very noisy congregational vote, it was decided to establish the future direction of our church. We received the go-ahead to merge the drive-in and the chapel congregations into one church on a new relocation development. This was indeed a most dramatic undertaking.

I was destined to have the unforgettable experience of being the pastor of a church during a major relocation experience. More than that, I was destined to be the pastor of a church that was split viciously down the middle. Those who opposed the merger and relocation were vehement. Secret meetings were held through the week. This went on for over two years.

Meeting opposition

For two years, I went to my study under the enormous weight of an awareness that nearly half of my people were violently opposed to the direction in which I was leading the church. For a period of a year and a half, I would have relished nothing more than a fatal heart attack. In that way, I would have been removed with honor from the unhappy scene! Nevertheless, we had to move ahead.

At this time, we had a net worth of approximately $10,000. A debt of $70,000—against total assets of $80,000. It was about then that we were given the opportunity to purchase ten acres of land a half-mile from the freeway, just west of the drive-in theater, at a price of $6600 an acre, or $66,000.

"I believe the owner will sell it to you for $18,000 down, and he'll take $400 a month to cover interest and principal until the entire property is paid for," a realtor informed us, adding: "If you're interested, we can open a 120-day escrow tomorrow with only $1000."

This proposal was first submitted to the church board and then, according to the practice we followed at that time, to the congregation. The congregation was consequently drawn into the entire nitty-gritty of discussing endless details in the process of arriving at a decision. In this way, we created a magnificent public platform for every negative thinker in the congregation to sound off and spread his negativism. Nevertheless, a motion was made and it barely passed, moving "that we purchase the ten acres of ground at the above price, open an escrow tomorrow for $1000, and instruct our pastor to close the escrow on or before the end of the 120-day period, providing he can raise the $18,000 down payment within the time allowed."

Raising funds   That kicked off the most intensive fund-raising project of my life—with the exception of raising the money for the first organ in my first church! I began by cashing in my life insurance policy and giving the proceeds to the church. I called my brother and talked him into loaning the money he had in his savings account to the church. I borrowed from my father, from my uncle, from my sister and from another uncle. We left no stone unturned!

Regrettably, nearly half the membership of the church was violently opposed to the entire project. Only about sixty people in all were actively behind the project at this stage! The others were doing all they could to kill it!

Suddenly, during this fund-raising period, property directly across the street from the piece of ground we were attempting to purchase was sold for $12,000 an acre— exactly double what we were asked to pay for ours! Clearly, we were on the right track.

I went now to Warren Gray, husband of Rosie, and he came through with a $2000 gift! Going into the final week of the 120-day period, I was only $3000 short of the full $18,000 that was needed!

The 120th day was scheduled to fall on a Friday. But there were still three people who had promised $1000 each. So I *knew* we had it made!

I went to the first man and he shocked me by reneging

166

on his offer. I went to the second. "Come back in a month—but right now, I'm flat broke." I was stunned.

Then I called on the third man—and he floored me by saying, "You know, Reverend, we just had my daughter's wedding. Do you know what that cost me? And my wife hasn't even balanced the checking account!" His voice trailed off in a ridiculous display of the kind of verbosity that flows out of a highly defensive mentality. I was sick!

Robert Moore, a faithful member of the church board, risked losing his job at Disneyland by spending the morning literally begging loans from his fellow employees. He called in to report that he'd collected $200. With that, every stone had been turned over and we were found wanting.

It was now Friday noon, and it looked like we were defeated! The escrow company's office was to close in only four more hours, and we were still $3000 short. The sellers would rejoice, of course, if we were unable to close this deal, for the selling of the property across the street now proved that they could easily get $120,000 for their land instead of the $66,000 we were offering. A great bargain was about to slip through our hands!

I went to a pay phone in Santa Ana, listened to the dime clink to the bottom, dialed my home phone and talked with my wife at the other end. With trembling lips, I reported failure.

"But you mustn't give up, honey," she insisted, adding, "Have you called Warren Gray?"

"I can't, dear," I insisted. "I can't ask a person to give twice!"

"Why not?" came her reply. "Besides, you'll have to tell him that you can give him his $2000 back!"

"But, honey, I can't call him today. He's only been home from the hospital a few days. You know they sewed him up full of cancer."

167

Again she insisted that I call his house. I did. The nurse gave him his telephone at his bedside. I explained to him that we failed to secure the down payment to close the escrow. "But we can keep the services going in the drive-in theater," I assured him.

"But, Reverend, you'll never get land near the freeway at that price again! You can't let the deal slide by. Give me a couple of hours and I'll meet you at the Bank of America at Eighth and Main," he said.

I objected, reminding him of his serious condition.

"But, Reverend, Rosie needs that land. And I've got the money for you if you can meet me at the bank." With that, he hung up.

Two hours later, I was pacing the floor of the Bank of America's lobby when I saw Warren come in, ashen-faced and hollow-eyed, his old rancher's hat topping his head of uncombed hair. He nodded to me, walked to a cashier's window, passed some papers to the girl behind the grill, and a few moments later confronted me in the center of the bank lobby with the sweat running off his face. "Here you are, Reverend, here's $3000," he said.

I shook his hand—hard. Then I went to the escrow company. *Sixty minutes before the deadline, God took title to His ten acres of land!*

The immediate crisis had been met. However, the opposition in the church was convinced that we would be going bankrupt. They had now cut off their financial support and we were barely able to make the payments on our little chapel. And now we would also have to start making payments of $400 a month on our newly-acquired land. A battle had been won, but the war continued.

Then, on the Sunday after the land cleared escrow, a deacon approached me, excitedly waving a check from an unknown family. "Reverend, look at this! A check for $100 from a stranger! If we got one of these every week, they would make our land payments!" The following week, another check for $100 came from the same party. And it has continued until this day!

What happened? Obviously, God wanted this church built. And He directed a family to our church whose tithe amounted to precisely the same amount as the land payment on the new property!

And why was the family attracted to our church? Because they heard that "The Garden Grove Community Church was announcing plans to build the world's first walk-in, drive-in church on ten acres of land on the east side of Garden Grove alongside the Santa Ana Freeway." That idea was big enough to excite these big-thinking people! And so they started coming at this precise moment in history!

Growing pains

Now we placed our lovely, three-year-old, stained-glass chapel in the lovely suburb up for sale! We sold it for approximately $40,000 more than we had invested in it. Why? Because it was the most beautiful church building in the village! Good architecture is always a great investment.

Then we hired Richard Neutra, considered the foremost living architect in the world at that time. Plans were drawn up for the walk-in, drive-in church. Finally, ground-breaking ceremonies were conducted.

The next morning, the Monday newspapers blared out the headlines: "Ground was broken yesterday for the world's first walk-in, drive-in church to be erected in Garden Grove, California. It will be the first church designed for people to sit outside and worship in their cars while others sit inside and worship in the traditional pew arrangement."

I was a happy man, except for the funeral that I had to conduct on that same afternoon. It was the funeral of Rosie Gray! God kept her alive through all of those years

169

until we were publicly committed to building the church that God wanted us to build.

Obviously, if God is in on the planning, money problems have a way of solving themselves! Probably that's the reason we dared to begin to plunge further into what some people would have called "debt." We calculated that we would have to borrow approximately $700,000 to build the first unit, complete with fountains, pools, landscaping and gardens. This would give us a sanctuary seating 1000 people, expandable to 1700 in the future. It would also give us a three-manual pipe organ.

Boosting income

We calculated that we could borrow the money at 6 percent interest. We assumed if we could boost our annual income to cover the interest on the $700,000 debt, even before we built the building, that the increased income generated by the new structure should help liquidate the principal indebtedness. But no commercial lending institution would loan us money.

We used professional fund-raisers instead. We conducted a campaign. We boosted our income well over $40,000 a year—enough to make the interest payments.

With that base established, we proceeded to borrow $700,000, offering only promissory notes as security. We approached members of our denominational family through our national periodical. It took us twenty-four months, but we succeeded!

Then on November 5, 1961, Dr. Norman Vincent Peale flew from New York City to dedicate the new Garden Grove Community Church, located just a half-mile west of the Orange Drive-In Theatre where he spoke for us five years before! We spent a few thousand dollars publicizing his presence in our church's services that day. Naturally, we had turn-away crowds. All of us were convinced this was a success!

Approximately four years later, I preached a sermon on "How to Make Your Dreams Come True" and launched my dream of someday building the main tower structure in the total church building plan. I announced that the architect and I envisioned a 14- or 15-story tower with high-speed glass elevators, a chapel at the top, a 24-hour telephone counseling center manned by live human beings every hour of every day; with offices for a growing church staff and a professional psychological counseling center, with the balance of the floors to be used for educational purposes.

I promised that the "little chapel in the sky at the top of the tower would be a twinkling diamond of hope in the black, night sky at the freeway hub of this great county." This tower would become a tower of hope representing and saying to the public that "there is an eye that never closes, there is an ear that is never shut, there is a heart that never grows cold."

The idea caught fire!

An "anonymous" donor started things off with $25. I announced to the congregation that a $25 contribution had been made and that the Tower of Hope fund had been opened! Someone else responded with a $50 gift! Twelve months later, the fund had grown to almost $6000.

About this time, someone said to me: "Reverend, at this rate you'll never get a million dollars." That challenged my imagination. I knew we were earning 6 percent interest on this $6000. Rising early one Sunday morning with pencil and paper, I scribbled out a rough calculation as to how long it would take $6000 earning 6 percent interest, compounded annually, to grow into a million dollars. I calculated it would take just a little over 100 years!

That Sunday I announced to the congregation: "I have good news for you! Sometime the Tower of Hope will stand here in the heart of Orange County! It will be a powerful positive statement of the light and love of Christ! We *really* have a million dollars right now. The only drawback is that we can't cash it in for 100 years!''

At this point, everyone knew that someday we would have a million dollars! The project became believable. Then the idea began to catch on and many people said they wanted to see it ''in their lifetime.''

''Is there any *possible* way we can raise a million dollars faster?'' That was the question people began asking. Well, perhaps if we broke it down in ten years, $100,000 a year would do it. And so we conducted a fund-raising campaign to boost our annual income by $100,000 a year, with pledges extended over a 10-year period to raise ''a million dollars for the Tower of Hope.''

The project was a success! True, the people could not, and would not, wait for ten years. The pressures grew to ''borrow the money and build it today.''

So we did!

By 1968, thirteen years after we organized and began services at the drive-in theater, Orange County's tallest structure stood completed! Telephones in the 24-hour counseling room at the top began ringing. An unbroken lifeline counseling program was started. The number was easy to remember. Dial: N-e-w H-o-p-e! So, Garden Grove Community Church became the first church in America to man a 24-hour live telephone counseling center.

By now, we had invested nearly $2 million in property, the original sanctuary, classrooms and the Tower of Hope. None of us suspected that a year and a half later we would plunge into another million-dollar project to purchase ten acres of additional land to provide desperately-needed parking space.

Setting goals   *Set goals beyond goals!*

Surely no one would ever have dreamed that before we reached our twentieth birthday we would be launching a 36-month capital funds campaign to raise another $1½ million preparing the financial base to build a larger 4000-seat auditorium. As this book goes to press the scale model is complete. Over $1 million is pledged and I hope that in the next three years the funding challenge will have been met and the great new cathedral erected. The existing 1700-seat sanctuary? It will be turned into one of America's largest church fellowship halls, seating 1500 around tables.

Let the unchurched population set your goals!

We are trying to live by our own principles. We could have elected not to build a larger sanctuary. But we have estimated there are one-half million unchurched people within a fifteen-minute driving radius from our church. Today we turn away people at 9:30 and again at 11:15 A.M.

We refuse to surrender leadership to our buildings. "The shoe must never tell the foot how big to grow," I told the congregation. They agreed.

As we are raising the money for the larger auditorium, we focus on the problem—the unchurched in the shadow of our cross! I am thanking everyone who is giving with this promise: "In our second twenty years thousands of desperate and despairing people will come here and find Christ—all because when you gave *you cared enough to make room for others.*"

Now—you make a decision to become a possibility thinker and dream great dreams for your great God!

Chapter 15

How You Can Dream Great Dreams

First of all, determine to succeed. Resolve now to believe in success. Christ was not a failure. He was a success, for He planned to live and die to be the sacrificial Saviour. Everything worked out exactly as He *planned* it. And in His parting words to His disciples, He urged them to *plan big plans* with the challenge, *go* "unto the uttermost part of the earth" (Acts 1:8).

How do possibility thinkers dream their dreams? Here's how—just follow these three steps as you plan, pray and prepare to become a great leader to build a great church for Jesus Christ:

1

Get in touch with God's Spirit. He has a dream for your life and your church. He will reveal His dream by causing you to desire what He wants. Prayerfully ask God to fill your life full with His Holy Spirit. To do this search your soul. Remove any secret or

176

public sin. Let nothing remain that could block the flow of God's Holy Spirit.

Now pray the prayer of surrender, "God I'm willing to do and be whatever you want me to be. I'm yours to command." Then ask the Holy Spirit to fill your mind with God's dream for your life.

Big beautiful dreams will come. If they are impossible then be sure they have come from God! If they're small and safe and entail no risk, the chances are they are of your own creation.

Let the big ideas come. Just because they're impossible doesn't mean God can't make it happen. Listen to this dream, "For it is God at work within you, giving you the will and the power to achieve His purpose" (Phil. 2:13, *Phillips*). Now...

Get in touch with God's people.

Show them your dream. God wants to use others, so they'll make it happen for you. It's His way of making sure that you'll remain humble after He starts showering success on your life!

My testimony is with the apostle Paul, "I can do all things through Christ" (Phil. 4:13). But I must also add, "I can't do anything without God's people."

Yes, God's people make the dreams come true! God has His people waiting in the wings to come out on stage at the right time, with the exact talent you'll need! There's someone out there with the skill or the will to remove the obstacles that will temporarily block your way!

Get in time with God's calendar.

Out of my first fifteen years' walk with God in building His church in Garden Grove I now share a lesson in prayer as I've learned it. I've talked in this book about faith, organizing, financing, planning. But believe me— before, during, and after every move there was deep,

177

constant prayer. And I testify that God always answers true prayer.

When the request is not right God says "no." I prayed for ten acres to build our church in downtown Garden Grove. God said *"no."* Three years later He showed us our present site—20 acres at the freeway hub of Orange County!

When you are not right God says, "Grow." It took me two dark years of depression, facing opposition in the church before I got the message. I had not really surrendered the church to Him. I had the idea that the Lord and Schuller were partners. The time came when He said, "The partnership is through—you work for Me!"

When the time is not right God says, "Slow." God's calendar is always right. Remember, God's delays are not God's denials. When you think you've failed you haven't. You just have to wait longer—work harder!

"Nothing is impossible," the Army Corps of Engineers used to say, "It just takes longer! Inch by inch anything's a cinch!" Faith is spelled P-A-T-I-E-N-C-E!

And when everything is right God says, "Go!" And doors will open. Dreams will come true. All because you decided to *bloom where you are planted.*

So, friend, dream your dreams and make them great! I have every confidence that you are about to turn a corner in your ministry, a turning with lasting, lifetime results. It is a turning that will take you from discouragement and near defeat to optimism and unexpected victories, from one level of success to another—to ever higher levels of accomplishment that you ever dreamed of before you started real possibility thinking!

Why am I so sure? Because the principles of success are all here. You've already read them. Now believe them and apply them. They will work, if you work them!

And if this is done, the Twentieth Century church in America will see a fantastic future unfold before it as it moves into the Twenty-First Century. And what will the future of the next century hold for all of the small churches in America?

1. Some small churches will begin to grow, will plan to relocate and will become tremendous centers of dynamic inspiration by Century 21.

2. Other small church will merge with other local small churches to do something big and beautiful for Christ in their city.

3. Other small, boxed-in churches will fold up and die! Some should!

4. Others will be sold to the city and community for branch libraries, child-care centers and other uses, while the nucleus moves out to a new 10- to 20-acre center!

5. Some reader of this book will build the greatest church ever built in America—a walk-in, drive-in church in blizzard country! With seven-days a week activity! It will be a sensation for Christ!

So—"Rise up, O men of God!
 The church for you doth wait;
 Her strength unequal to her task—
 Rise up and make her great!"
    —William P. Merrill

The contents of this book are based on lectures given by Dr. Robert H. Schuller at his Institute for Successful Church Leadership.

To receive information on these four-day seminars, write to:
Wilbert Eichenberger
R.H.S. Institute
12141 Lewis Street
Garden Grove, California 92640

To receive copies of morning messages delivered by Dr. Schuller, write to:
Dr. Robert Schuller
Hour of Power
Garden Grove, California 92640